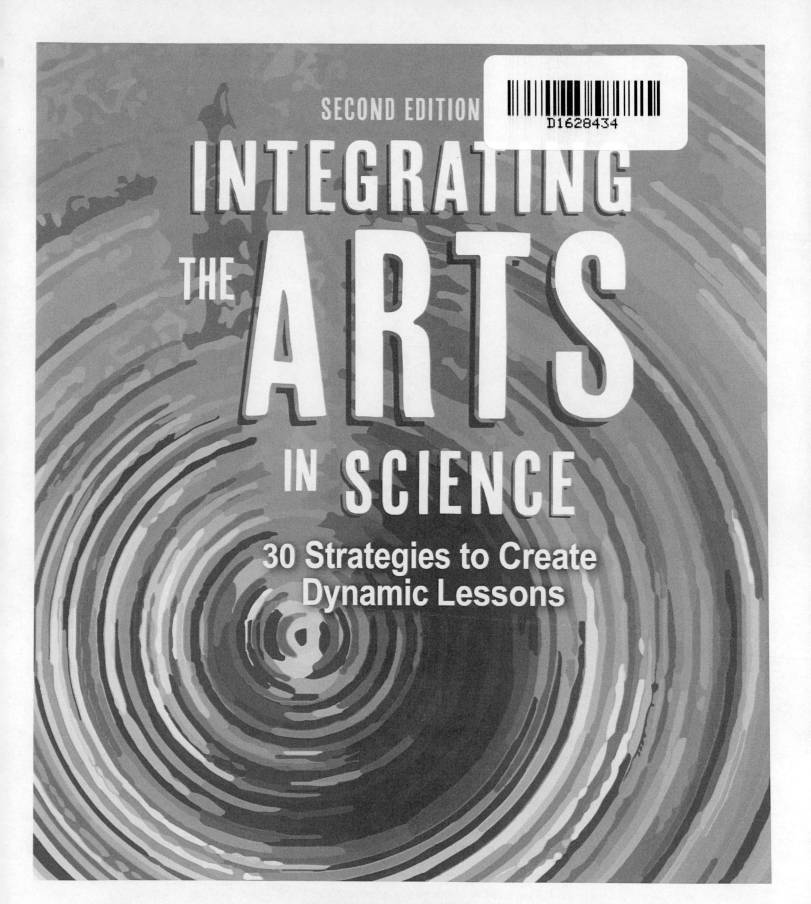

SECOND EDITION

INTEGRATING THE ARTS IN SCIENCE

30 Strategies to Create Dynamic Lessons

Vivian Poey, M.F.A.
Nicole Weber, Ph.D.
Gene Diaz, Ph.D.
Sam Smiley, M.F.A.

Contributing Authors

Lisa Donovan, Ph.D., Professor, Massachusetts College of Liberal Arts, Fine and Performing Arts

Alyson Marcel, Graduate Student, Master's in Art Therapy at Lesley University

Celeste Miller, M.F.A., Choreographer, Associate Professor of Dance, Grinnell College

Louise Pascale, Ph.D., Professor Emerita, Creative Arts in Learning, Lesley University

Dana Schildkraut, Arts Integration Specialist, Berkshire Regional Arts Integration Network, Massachusetts College of Liberal Arts

Consultants

William Barowy, Ph.D., Associate Professor of Science and Technology in Education Programs, Lesley University

Meg Lippert, Director of Storytelling, Homer Learning, and Adjunct Faculty, Creative Arts in Learning, Lesley University

Katina McClain, Doctoral Student, Lesley University

Publishing Credits

Corinne Burton, M.A.Ed., *Publisher*
Aubrie Nielsen, M.S.Ed., *EVP of Content Development*
Véronique Bos, *Creative Director*
Cathy Hernandez, *Senior Content Manager*
Laureen Gleason, *Editor*
David Slayton, *Assistant Editor*

Image Credits: All images from iStock Photo and/or Shutterstock

Standards

NGSS Lead States. 2013. *Next Generation Science Standards: For States, By States*. Washington, DC: The National Academies Press.
© Copyright 2010 National Governors Association Center for Best Practices and Council of Chief State School Officers. All rights reserved.
© Copyright 2007–2021 Texas Education Agency (TEA). All Rights Reserved.
National Core Arts Standards © 2015 National Coalition for Core Arts Standards. All rights reserved.

A Division of Teacher Created Materials
5482 Argosy Avenue
Huntington Beach, CA 92649-1039
www.tcmpub.com/shell-education
ISBN 978-0-7439-7023-5
© 2022 Shell Educational Publishing, Inc.

Table of Contents

Preface

Welcome to the second edition of the Integrating the Arts series! Now more than ever educators are experiencing what the arts have always accomplished: instructional approaches for social emotional learning and culturally responsive teaching that value students' funds of knowledge and lived experiences.

This series was launched initially to take the success of arts integration in transforming classrooms and to share it more widely, foregrounding effective and easy-to-implement ideas. Since then, educators reached out to us to share their success stories using strategies from the first edition. Here in our second edition we offer even more learning experiences for your classroom.

We're so grateful for the feedback we received from educators about the first edition of this series. We loved hearing how you could flip through the books with your colleagues at planning time and choose a lesson to implement that afternoon or the next day. The practical aspect of the books was a highlight of the feedback. We learned that the lessons were versatile and worked with a wide variety of topics and learning targets. You'll find this continues to be a focus in our latest work.

. . . .

"The arts help children develop creative problem-solving skills, motor skills, language skills, social skills, decision-making skills, risk-taking skills, and inventiveness."

—Sharuna Segaren
(2019, para. 20)

. . . .

Here's what you'll find new and different in the second edition:

- inclusion of diverse perspectives and culturally responsive strategies that invite students to tap into their individual ideas and lived experiences

- a variety of student examples

- carefully selected ideas for mentor texts of multiple genres and modalities

- suggestions for the inclusion of primary sources

- several new strategies to bring to your classroom

- call-out boxes to highlight key insights and ideas

- resources for finding texts that bring diverse voices to your classroom

- a new structure in the movement chapter that provides additional details for classroom implementation

- a focus on the elements and key vocabulary of each art form

- updated standards

Dig in and enjoy! Let the power and novelty of the arts bolster deep engagement with your content areas. We hope you create, experiment, and explore the artistic strategies alongside students, curating your own portfolio of creative work.

The Importance of Arts Integration

Study after study points to compelling evidence of the significant outcomes linked to arts integration. According to the President's Committee on the Arts and the Humanities, "Studies have now documented significant links between arts integration models and academic and social outcomes for students, efficacy for teachers, and school-wide improvements in culture and climate. Arts integration is efficient, addressing a number of outcomes at the same time. Most important, the greatest gains in schools with arts integration are often seen school-wide and also with the most hard-to-reach and economically disadvantaged students" (2011, 19). According to the New Jersey Arts Integration Think and Do Workbook, "The key benefits of arts integration primarily fall into four categories: Improving student academic achievement, student social emotional development, teacher practice, and classroom culture" Bruce et al. (2020, 21). Now more than ever, integrating the arts into our teaching creates opportunities for deep engagement and connection and an opportunity for our students to find relevance in course content to their lives.

The Ford Foundation funded a study led by researchers from Lesley University's Creative Arts in Learning Division and an external advisory team. The study involved research with more than two hundred Lesley alumni teaching across the country who had been trained in arts-integration strategies. Findings from the study suggest that arts-integrated teaching provides students with a variety of strategies for accessing content and expressing understanding of what they have learned that is culturally responsive and relevant to their lives. This leads to deep learning, increased student ownership, and engagement with academic content. Not only does arts integration engage students in creativity, innovation, and imagination, it renews teachers' commitment to teaching (Bellisario and Donovan with Prendergast 2012).

> "The key benefits of arts integration fall into four categories: improving student academic achievement, student social emotional development, teacher practice, and classroom culture."
>
> —Eloise Bruce et al. (2020, 21)

Really then, the question becomes this: How can we provide students with access to the arts as an engaging way to learn and express ideas across the curriculum?

Arts integration is the investigation of curricular content through artistic explorations, where the arts provide an avenue for rigorous investigation, representation, expression, and reflection of both curricular content and the art form itself (Diaz, Donovan, and Pascale 2006). This book provides teachers with concrete strategies to integrate the arts across the curriculum. Arts-integration strategies are introduced with contextual information about the art form (storytelling, drama, poetry, music, visual arts, and creative movement).

The Importance of Arts Integration *(cont.)*

Each art form provides you with innovative strategies to help students fully engage with and connect to different content areas. Storytelling connects us with our roots in the oral tradition and can heighten students' awareness of the role of story in their lives. Drama challenges students to explore multiple perspectives of characters, historical figures, and scientists. Poetry invites students to build a more playful, fresh relationship with written and spoken language. Music develops students' ability to listen, generate a sense of community, and communicate and connect aurally. Visual art taps into students' ability to observe critically, envision, think through metaphor, and build visual literacy in a world where images are pervasive. Creative movement encourages students to embody ideas and work conceptually.

Providing students with the opportunity to investigate curriculum and express their understanding with the powerful languages of the arts will deepen their understanding, heighten their curiosity, and bring forward their voices as they interact more fully with content and translate their ideas into new forms. This book is a beginning, a "way in."

We invite you to see all of this for yourself by bringing the strategies shared in this book to your classroom and watching what happens. We hope this resource leaves you looking for deeper experiences with the arts for both you and your students.

> "Early-career teachers attribute much of their differentiation ability to the arts-integration class. They also report the joy it brings to both teaching and learning, even within a crowded instructional day."
>
> —Jamie Hipp and Margaret-Mary Sulentic Dowell (2021, para. 8)

What Does It Mean to Integrate the Arts?

We believe that a vital element necessary in establishing a learning environment that fosters artistic creativity and evokes scientific curiosity and exploration can be found in the integration of the arts and science. Active involvement in the arts can help learners in science and other fields explore different perspectives and internalize new ideas and ways of thinking.

The beauty of the world that we know through the study of science is often missing in our lessons as we share information and require students to engage in the scientific method as a mandate. When we integrate science with the arts in our teaching, learning becomes multisensory, gains relevance, and we add joy to the experience. Students build on their own curiosity. The arts provide a vivid and dynamic context in which learners can wrestle with scientific ideas, scientific methods, and scientific reasoning.

You might think that engagement with the arts and the sciences is reserved for the few who have been given special gifts, those who have rare expertise. But this is not the case—you do not need to be an artist or a scientist to add this teaching approach to your repertoire. While we encourage collaboration with arts specialists

The Importance of Arts Integration (cont.)

across disciplines and grade levels, we also want to emphasize this point. No special abilities or talents are needed except for the willingness to begin!

There are many connections between the arts and the sciences. For example, architects, sculptors, and musicians must rely on scientific knowledge every day in physics, chemistry, biology, and Earth sciences. There are times in the science classroom when the arts are used to introduce or culminate the study of a specific topic. Some teachers may already have favorite lessons in which mobile sculptures become solar systems or lessons in which children learn to dance the growth of a tree. What we are aiming for here, though, is a seamless blending of the two areas in a sustained manner. We will guide you in the use of the arts and provide a context in which scientific concepts take shape and deepen while the arts inform and enrich the lives of your students. This is not just for enrichment but also for a change in practice that allows you to create your own path into arts integration. We want you to use arts integration as an approach to teaching the most prevalent standards in your science curriculum and to do so frequently. When scientific ideas are taught through artistic explorations, students develop skills and knowledge in both disciplines. We will share strategies with you that are flexible enough to be used across content strands and grade levels.

With our current curricula dominated by reading and mathematics, little room is left for the arts and sciences. Yet as educators, we want to teach the whole child. Students need both the arts and academic disciplines. Research suggests that academic achievement may be linked to the arts (Kennedy 2006). As noted by Douglas Reeves (2007), "the challenge for school leaders is to offer every student a rich experience with the arts without sacrificing the academic opportunities students need" (80). By integrating the arts with the sciences, we are able to place

scientific ideas within rich settings *and* provide our students with access to the arts.

> "The arts can lead to 'deep learning' in which students are more engaged with academic content, spend more time on task, and take ownership of their learning."
>
> —Kerrie Bellisario and Lisa Donovan with Monica Prendergast (2012)

Why Should I Integrate the Arts?

Mathematics and science are frequently linked together in schools, with STEM (Science, Technology, Engineering, and Mathematics) initiatives formalizing this association. While we applaud STEM efforts, we seek to expand the potential for other interdisciplinary connections. The arts also offer particular advantages for learning that should not be ignored. In a briefing on changing STEM to STEAM with the inclusion of the arts, John Maeda, former president of the Rhode Island School of Design, noted that STEM would benefit by adding the arts and design to trigger more innovation (Rhode Island School of Design 2011). Beth Baker (2012) states that "innovation happens through science, technology, engineering, and mathematics. Could it be missing something that is actually quite important? It's missing the arts—the right-brain innovation that has propelled our country, made us competitive" (253).

The Importance of Arts Integration *(cont.)*

Rinne et al. (2011) identify several ways in which arts integration improves long-term retention through elaboration, enactment, and rehearsal. Specifically, when learners create and add details to their own visual models, dramatize a concept or skill, sing a song repeatedly, or rehearse for a performance, they increase the likelihood that they will remember what they have learned. This retention lasts over time, not just after the span of the unit. Through arts integration, students eagerly revisit, review, rehearse, edit, and work through ideas repeatedly and in authentic ways as they translate ideas into new forms.

As brain research deepens our understanding of how learning takes place, educators have come to better appreciate the importance of the arts. The arts support communication, emotional connections, community, and higher-order thinking. They also are linked to increased academic achievement, especially among at-risk students. Eric Jensen (2001) argues that "the arts enhance the process of learning. The systems they nourish, which include our integrated sensory, attentional, cognitive, emotional, and motor capabilities, are, in fact, the driving forces behind all other learning." Lessons and activities that integrate science and the arts provide a rich environment in which all students can explore scientific ideas—particularly those students who need new ways to access curriculum and express understanding. These lessons and activities also provide another source of motivation.

Teaching through the arts provides authentic differentiated learning for every student in the classroom. As former director of Harvard's Mind, Brain, and Education program Todd Rose (2012) notes, all learners learn in variable ways. The Center for Applied Special Technology (n.d.) suggests that in meeting the needs of variable learners, educators should expand their teaching to provide universal design. That is, teachers should include strategies that "are flexible and responsive to the needs of all learners"

by providing "multiple means of engagement, methods of presentation of content and multiple avenues for expression of understanding." The integration of the arts provides opportunities to address all three universal design principles.

For example, the process of enacting a scene from a text provides a meaningful opportunity for metacognition, or "what a child knows about [their] own thinking and how the child is able to monitor that thinking" (Yellin, Jones, and DeVries 2007). Imagine students who, as they prepare to enact a scene from a book, determine what parts of the reading are unclear, go back through the text and reread, visualize the events, and visualize themselves performing the scene. Arts integration benefits students not only by deepening their connection to content and fostering interdisciplinary learning in the arts and science but also by promoting what Partnership for 21st Century Learning (2019) researchers note as the 4 Cs: creativity, critical thinking, communication, and collaboration. Arts integration brings these significant benefits to learning and engages teachers and students in curiosity, imagination, and passion for learning.

Arts and the Standards

Essential Qualities of a Science Program

The National Research Council of the National Academies (National Research Council 2012) states that science teaching and learning are powerful when built around three major dimensions:

1. Scientific and engineering practices
2. Crosscutting concepts
3. Core ideas within four disciplinary areas (physical science; life science; Earth and space science; and engineering, technology, and application of science)

The science and engineering practices reflect how professionals work in the field and directly relate to artistic processes. The crosscutting concepts further aid in providing an organizational framework that helps students connect interdisciplinary knowledge in a meaningful way to understand the world from a scientific point of view. These concepts include patterns; cause and effect; scale, proportion, and quantity; systems and system models; energy and matter; structure and function; and stability and change. We believe that integration with the arts supports a deeper understanding of the general science practices, crosscutting concepts, and content knowledge within the local environmental context where possible. The model lessons in this book were developed with these goals in mind.

Arts and the Standards *(cont.)*

Artistic Habits of Mind

In addition to experiencing essential qualities of science programs, students will be developing artistic habits of mind (Hetland et al. 2007). With these habits of mind, students will be able to:

1. Develop craft
2. Engage and persist
3. Envision
4. Express
5. Observe
6. Reflect
7. Stretch and explore
8. Understand the art world

Although these habits were identified in an investigation of visual arts practices, they are relevant for the practice of all the arts. As students engage in science through these lenses, their understanding will deepen. They will become active participants in making meaning, discussing ideas, and reflecting on their learning.

The skills that the arts develop are valued in every field. The arts develop these skills naturally as students explore and translate ideas into artistic forms. Researcher Lois Hetland notes that "it is these qualities—intrinsic to the arts—that are valued in every domain but not necessarily taught in those subjects in school. That's what makes the arts such potent resources for teaching valued dispositions—what the arts teach well is not used uniquely in the arts but is valuable across a wide spectrum of contexts" (2009, 37).

Classroom Environment

Whether you are in a virtual learning space or face-to-face, a safe classroom environment is vital for scientific ideas and artistic expressions to flourish. Learners must feel comfortable to

make mistakes, critique the work of others, and celebrate success. Think back to groups to which you have presented new ideas or creative works. How did you feel as you waited for their reactions? What was it about their behavior that made you feel more or less comfortable? What was it about your thinking that made you feel more or less safe? Such reflections will lead you to ways you can help students feel more comfortable sharing their ideas. As teachers we must be role models for our students as we model our willingness to take risks and engage in new ways of learning. You will find that the arts by their nature invite risk taking, experimentation, and self-discipline, as well as encourage the development of a supportive learning community.

Developing a learning community in which learners support and respect one another takes time, but there are things you can do to help support its development:

■ **Establish clear expectations for respect.** Respect is nonnegotiable. As students engage in creative explorations, it is crucial that they honor one another's ideas, invite all voices to the table, and discuss the work in ways

Arts and the Standards *(cont.)*

that value each contribution. Self-discipline and appreciation for fellow students' creative work are often beneficial outcomes of arts integration (Bellisario and Donovan with Prendergast 2012). Take time for students to brainstorm ways in which they can show one another respect and react when they feel they have not been respected. Work with students to create guidelines for supporting the creative ideas of others and agree to uphold them as a group.

- **Explore several icebreakers** during the first weeks of school that encourage students to get to know one another informally and begin to discover interests they have in common. As students learn more about one another, they develop a sense of themselves as individuals and as a classroom unit and are more apt to want to support one another. Using fun, dynamic warm-ups not only helps students get their brains working but also builds a sense of community and support for risk taking.

- **Tell students the ways in which you are engaged in learning new ideas.** Talk about your realizations and challenges along the way, and demonstrate your own willingness to take risks and persevere.

- **Find ways to support the idea that we all can act, draw, sing, rhyme, and so forth.** Avoid saying negative things about your own arts or science skill levels, and emphasize your continuous growth.

- **Draw out students' ideas by asking open-ended questions.** Ask how, why, in what ways? These prompts encourage students to articulate, refocus, or clarify their own thinking.

- **Encourage risk-taking.** Give students the experiences they need to build confidence and express themselves in new ways. Encourage students to reflect on their own goals and whether they think they have met them.

- **Emphasize process over product.** Enormous learning and discovery take place during the creative process. This is as significant as the final product and often even more so.

How This Book Is Organized

Strategies

The strategies and model lessons in this book are organized within six art modalities:

1. Storytelling
2. Drama
3. Poetry
4. Music
5. Visual Arts
6. Creative Movement

Within each modality, five strategies are presented that integrate that art form with the teaching of science. The strategies are not intended as an exhaustive list but rather as exemplary ways to integrate the arts into the sciences.

Although we have provided a model lesson for each strategy, these strategies are flexible and can be used in a variety of ways across a variety of content areas. These models will give you the opportunity to try out the ideas with students and envision many other ways to adapt these strategies for use in your teaching. For example, in the drama strategy of teacher in role, we emphasize design engineering of transportation, but you may prefer to integrate it with other areas of science or STEM, such as cell biology (where the teacher takes on the role of a cell biologist) or geology. The strategy of found poetry can be used to explore primary source letters, photographs, oral histories, the environment around us, and more. As you become more familiar and comfortable with the strategies, you may combine a variety of them across the art modalities within one lesson. For example, you might have students begin with creative movement to explore organic materials, then dramatize experts in the field finding examples of organic materials and listing the terms and characteristics they associate with those materials, and finally use those words as "found words" to write a poem. The goal is to make the choices that best fit you and your students.

How This Book Is Organized *(cont.)*

Organization of the Lessons

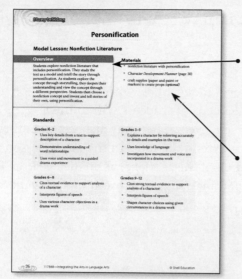

Each model lesson begins with an **overview**, followed by the list of standards addressed. Note that the standards involve equal rigor for both science and the arts.

A list of **materials** you will need is provided.

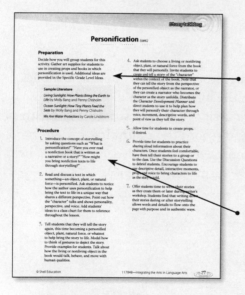

A **preparation** section follows with ways you can better ensure a successful learning investigation. Ideas may relate to grouping students, using props to engage learners, or practicing readings with dramatic flair.

The **procedure** section provides step-by-step directions on how to implement the model lesson.

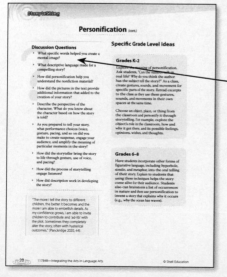

Each model lesson includes **questions** that you can ask as students work. The questions serve to highlight students' reasoning in science, stimulate their artistic thinking, or debrief their experience.

How This Book Is Organized (cont.)

Organization of the Lessons (cont.)

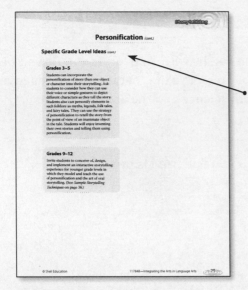

Specific grade-level ideas follow with suggestions on how to better meet the needs of students within the K–2, 3–5, 6–8, and 9–12 grade levels. They may also suggest others ways to explore or extend the ideas in the model lesson at these levels. Read all of the sections, as an idea written for a different grade span may suggest something you want to do with students.

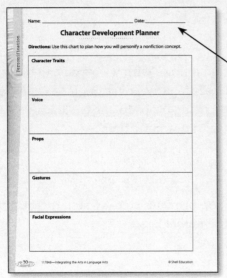

Reproducibles are provided for all applicable model lessons. Often in the form of graphic organizers, the reproducibles are designed to help students brainstorm ideas, organize and record their thinking, or reflect on their learning. Reproducibles are also available as digital downloads in PDF form (see page 256).

How This Book Is Organized (cont.)

How to Use the Lessons

These strategies can be used to teach science in any K–12 classroom with any science curriculum. A strategy lesson can be implemented as a way to deepen or expand the exploration of a topic or, if you have the flexibility, expanded to several days or a week. You may choose to use the strategy lesson within your science lesson, in combination with time assigned to the arts, or when considering storytelling or poetry, perhaps in conjunction with other content areas.

You may wish to focus on one art form at a time in order to become familiar with using that art modality to teach knowledge and skills in science as well as the art form being employed. Or you may want to look through the content index and explore models that relate to what you are teaching now or are about to teach. Over time, you will become familiar with the strategies and find that you choose to integrate them on a regular basis. If integrating arts and science is new to you, consider working with another teacher to explore the ideas together. Collaborate with teachers of art, dance, drama, or music in your school system to draw from their expertise in deepening the artistic work.

Working with Text Sets

We know the power of mentor texts and have recommended books that work well with particular strategies within each lesson, and we also encourage you to draw from a variety of texts such as newspapers, web-based resources, and primary and secondary sources. Think of artistic work as text, as it provides worlds to be explored (e.g., painting, musical scores, plays, choreographed work, and poems). This gives students the opportunity to engage with a variety of complex texts. Engaging in the arts promotes the kind of "close reading" that complex text requires (Varlas 2012).

For each lesson, we encourage working with text sets and resources from multiple genres and modalities. Cappiello and Dawes (2013) discuss "multimodal, multigenre" text sets, explaining that a text set draws from various modalities, including print, audio, photographs, artifacts, webcams, and podcasts. By multigenre, they suggest diverse forms of writing, such as blogs, in addition to traditional genres, such as books and magazines. Text sets may include nonfiction, fiction, poetry, and more to present a wide view of one topic and the approaches of multiple authors.

The recommended resources on the following page are filled with book suggestions and ideas.

How This Book Is Organized (cont.)

Recommended Resources

1. National Science Foundation Classroom Resources

www.nsf.gov/news/classroom/

The National Science Foundation offers a rich collection of lessons and resources. The materials are arranged by research areas and include biology, chemistry, the environment, engineering, physics, and more.

2. Outstanding Science Trade Books

www.nsta.org/outstanding-science-trade-books-students-k-12

This website for K-12 educators provides an annual list of outstanding children's science trade books, selected by a review panel appointed by the National Science Teacher's Association. The books include traditional science content as well as books related to engineering and design.

3. International Storytelling Center

www.storytellingcenter.net/

Begun by a teacher in Tennessee in 1972, the Storytelling Center celebrates the oral tradition of storytelling practiced around the world and across many cultures. In their Learning Library you will find Story Guides for the classroom to accompany footage from the National Storytelling Festival, an annual event, as well as many other resources ideal for young learners in grades 3-12. "Telling Stories that Matter" offers you a toolkit for exploring your own potential as a storyteller. And "Exploring the Power of Story" features an interview with Navajo Code Talker Peter MacDonald and includes the Freedom Stories Project and a specially curated list of Storytelling TED Talks. The Center's collection of videos and other resources is worth a visit as you explore the power of storytelling.

4. Academy of American Poets

www.poets.org

This incredible website features a wide variety of poems and poets; *Poem-a-Day; National Poetry Month; American Poets* magazine; and many resources geared specifically toward teachers, including *Teach This Poem* and *Materials for Teachers*. Be sure to watch the video called "A Teacher's Guide to Poets.org," in which Richard Blanco—poet and education ambassador for the Academy of American Poets—shares an inspiring talk to welcome you into the world of resources on this website.

5. Poetry Foundation

www.poetryfoundation.org

Here you will find a wide variety of poems, poets, collections, *Poem of the Day*, articles, podcasts, videos, and more. For example, the collection called *Poems on Immigration* includes the topics of immigration and immigrant life, poems about refugees and exile, poems on borders and crossings, articles, audio, and video. In the "History and Mission" section of this invaluable website, the independent organization seeks to "discover and celebrate the best poetry and to place it before the largest possible audience." The Poetry Foundation also publishes *Poetry* magazine.

6. NASA for Educators

www.nasa.gov/stem/foreducators/k-12/index.html

Founded in 1953, the National Aeronomics and Space Administration (NASA) has compiled a wide range of complimentary resources for educators. These include virtual field trips, STEM resources, NASAtv, and a blog about NASA projects. Teachers will find material to engage their students in topics such as history of women in space, science in space, and more.

How This Book Is Organized (cont.)

7. National Geographic for Educators

www.nationalgeographic.org/education

National Geographic offers a wide array of opportunities to learn for "educators engaging with students from pre-K to post-secondary." Programs and resources range from in-the-field projects to digital resources to online networks to grant opportunities and courses.

8. National Oceanic and Atmospheric Administration

www.noaa.gov/education

The National Oceanic and Atmospheric Administration (NOAA) "provides essential information on climate and change, not only in the United States, but throughout the world." The site serves as a clearinghouse of teaching and learning resources on our oceans and atmosphere. There are resources for educators and learners of all levels.

9. Google Arts and Culture

artsandculture.google.com

This global resource brings art from over two thousand museums to your laptop. The site includes virtual tours of museums, exhibitions, and artist collections. We especially appreciate the quick access to diverse artists and traditions that can fuel student research, provide rich artistic work to enhance any curriculum, and enhance a variety of teaching resources.

10. Jacob's Pillow Archives: Dance Interactive and Online Database

www.jacobspillow.org/archives

This robust offering of online archives, videos, essays, and podcasts documents the history of dance at Jacob's Pillow. The site provides access to "documentation of the ongoing activities of Jacob's Pillow and Audience Engagement programing" including exhibitions and talks that explore various aspects of dance history. We especially appreciate access to footage of dance through the Jacob's Pillow Dance Interactive. This resource documents "hundreds of artists who have appeared at the Pillow from the 1930s to the present day, . . . and offers carefully-chosen excerpts from the Archives' extensive video collection accompanied by contextual information, plus an extensive section of multimedia essays that include talks, photos, and other exclusive content organized into various themes."

How This Book Is Organized (cont.)

Assessment

"Data-driven decision-making," "documentation of learning," and "meeting benchmarks" are all phrases that refer to assessment practices embedded in our schools. Assessment has become a time-consuming activity for all involved in education, and yet the time and effort spent does not always yield what is needed to improve learning. As you think about how to assess lessons and activities that integrate science and the arts, it is important to stop and consider how to best use assessment to increase learning for students. Chances are that in addressing that goal you also will be documenting learning in ways that can be shared with students, parents, administrators, and other interested stakeholders.

We encourage you to focus on formative assessment—that is, assessment that is incorporated throughout the process of learning. This assessment will inform your instructional decisions during the process of teaching. The purpose of this assessment is to provide feedback for learners and teachers along the way, in addition to feedback to at the end. As such, we are interested in the data we collect during the learning process as well as after it is completed. The goals are to make the learning process visible, to determine the depth of understanding, and to note the process the students undergo as they translate their scientific knowledge into an art form or explore scientific ideas through the arts.

There are a variety of tools you can use to gather data to support your instructional decision-making:

- **Ask questions to draw out, clarify, and probe students' thinking.** The questions in each strategy section will provide you with ideas on which you can elaborate. Use questioning to make on-the-spot adjustments to your plans as well as to identify learning

moments as they are unfolding. This can be as simple as posing a new question or as complex as bringing a few students together for a mini-lesson.

- **Walk around with a clipboard or notebook to capture students' comments and your own observations.** Too often we think we will remember students' words only to find ourselves unable to reproduce them at a later time. These annotations will allow you to note patterns within a student's remarks or among students' comments. They can suggest misconceptions that provide you with an entry to the next day's work. For example, you might share a comment such as, "Yesterday I noticed that your monologues suggested motivations for your historical figures in science that were different from what the texts have shared. Let's talk about how this might be possible based on the sources we have and what you have learned about how history is written."

- **Use the graphic organizers in the model lessons** as support for the creative process. Using these forms, have students brainstorm ideas for their artistic process and their science connections. These organizers provide a snapshot of students' thinking at various points in the creative process and create opportunities for teachers to collect evidence of their learning from various perspectives (student planning, reflection and synthesis, peer review, and teacher observation) as well as documentation at different stages of the learning process (planning, implementation of ideas, review of work, revision, and so on).

- **Use a camera to document student learning.** Each of the strategies leads to a creative product but not necessarily one that provides a tangible artifact or one that fits on a standard sheet of paper. Use a digital

How This Book Is Organized (cont.)

camera to take numerous pictures that can capture, for example, a piece of visual art at various stages of development or the gestures actors and storytellers use in their dramatic presentations. Similarly, use video to capture planning sessions, group discussions, and final presentations. In addition to documenting learning, collecting such evidence helps students reflect back on their learning. Consider developing a learning portfolio for students that they can review and add to over time.

- **Recognize that each strategy not only leads to a final creative product, but the creative processes leading to final work are laden with evidence of learning.** Comparisons can be made across products to note student growth.

- **Make students an integral part of the assessment process.** Provide students with opportunities to reflect on their work. For example, have students choose artifacts to include in their portfolio and explain the reasons for their choices. Have students reflect on their work as a class. Encourage discussion of artistic work to not only draw out what students have learned in their own creative process but also how and what they learned from the work of their peers. In this way students teach and learn from one another.

- **Design rubrics that help you organize your assessment data.** A well-crafted rubric can help you gather data more quickly as well as increase the likelihood that you are being equitable in your evaluation of assessment data. Select criteria to assess learning in science as well as in the art form, because arts integration supports equal rigor both in content and in the arts.

Arts integration deepens learning both in the content area being explored and in the art form being used. To give you an example of how you could use these strategies in the classroom, consider the collaborative storytelling strategy. In an architecture studio at the Children's Studio School in Washington, DC, students ranging in age from four to six years old investigated water. They looked at water from various perspectives, including where it comes from, how it gets to us, what it is used for, and how the water cycle works. In Vivian Poey's visual art studio, students investigated the systems at work in getting us what we need. Students immediately brought up water, which had been a big part of their previous learning. As a way of assessing what students already understood about water, the teacher invited students to develop a collaborative story that applied their knowledge in a fantastic fictional account based on what would happen if Earth's water disappeared.

As students sat in a circle, the teacher provided the beginning of the story: "Once there was an enormous bird flying in outer space. His nose was dry, and his throat was dry. He was so frustrated that he came to Earth's atmosphere and breathed up all the clouds. Every time the sun evaporated more water, the bird would inhale it again, trying to wet his nose. So the water did not come down." The teacher then invited students to continue that thread to develop the story. One student began, "Down on Earth, there was a boy who had wings. His name was Fred. His arms were inside the wings. He was wearing wingmitts, like mittens, but he had wings. But it was not cold; he was just wearing them because he likes to." The story continued to unfold as each individual student added a line:

> *"Fred was flying, and his nose was dry, and his throat was dry."*
> *"It was in the sky in the daytime."*
> *"He keeps sniffing and sniffing because no rain is coming."*
> *"His feathers fell because the rain didn't come down."*
> *"The plants died."*

How This Book Is Organized *(cont.)*

"He ate nothing."
"He was going to die."
"He was looking poorer and poorer and poorer,
and soon he had no food."
"He realizes that all the plants and the leaves on the tree are gone. And then he goes back and he knows where this is all coming from, and he worries it will go on forever."
"Fred took a feather from the bird, and he tickled his nose and the bird sneezed all the water out."
"The water went down the drain."
"The plants growed and growed and growed until they were tall as trees."
"The bird sneezed more water out."
"And the grass growed."
"And Fred's nose got wetter and his throat got clearer and clearer and clearer."
"He flew up in the sky."
"And he ate the grass."
"And he flew up all the way to the clouds."
"And there was never anyone thirsty again."
"And the bird left and went with his family to celebrate because he found home. There is a waterfall and it also rains a lot because it is always spring."
"The end of our book."

In this story, students independently created a main character and took the story to the moment of crisis and through to resolution. The story reflects not only what the students know about water (plants need it to grow and therefore humans need it to drink and also to eat) but also what they know about the structure of stories. In this case, the collaborative storytelling strategy was used as a quick pre-assessment before entering a conversation about systems. It established a good starting point for the conversation and the work to come. Students could then move from the fictional and fantastic to a factual investigation about the complex systems at work. In this case, the questions to ask and investigate can come directly from the story:

Why did the plants die? Why do we need plants? How do plants get their water? How do we get our water? Where does our water come from?

As there are so many aspects of this task to capture, a rubric can be quite helpful. A suggested rubric is provided in the Digital Resources (see page 256). Observation protocols help teachers document evidence of student learning, something all teachers must do. A variety of forms could be used, and it is not possible to include all areas that you might attend to in an interdisciplinary lesson. Two suggested forms are included in the Digital Resources (see page 256). For more guidance on assessment, see *Integrating the Arts Across the Curriculum, Second Edition*, by Lisa Donovan and Louise Pascale (2022).

Correlation to the Standards

Shell Education is committed to producing educational materials that are research and standards based. To support this effort, this resource is correlated to the academic standards of all 50 United States, the District of Columbia, the Department of Defense Dependent Schools, and the Canadian provinces. A correlation is also provided for key professional development organizations.

How to Find Standards Correlations

To print a customized correlation report for your state, visit our website at **www.tcmpub.com /administrators/correlations** and follow the online directions. If you require assistance in printing correlation reports, please contact the Customer Service Department at 1-800-858-7339.

Purpose and Intent of Standards

The Every Student Succeeds Act (ESSA) mandates that all states adopt challenging academic standards that help students meet the goal of college and career readiness. While many states already adopted academic standards prior to ESSA, the act continues to hold states accountable for detailed and comprehensive standards. Standards are designed to focus instruction and guide adoption of curricula. They define the knowledge, skills, and content students should acquire at each level. Standards also are used to develop standardized tests to evaluate students' academic progress. State standards are used in the development of our resources, so educators can be assured they meet state academic requirements.

College and Career Readiness

Today's college and career readiness (CCR) standards offer guidelines for preparing K–12 students with the knowledge and skills necessary to succeed in postsecondary job training and education. CCR standards include the Common Core State Standards as well as other state-adopted standards, such as the Texas Essential Knowledge and Skills. The standards listed on the lessons describe the content presented throughout the lessons.

Storytelling

Storytelling

Understanding Storytelling

Storytelling has been part of every culture since the beginning of time (Norfolk, Stenson, and Williams 2006). Stories have been used to educate, inspire, and entertain. There is the story itself, and then there is the telling of the tale by a skilled teller. Storytellers use language, gesture, eye contact, tone, and inflection as they share a story with an audience. A good storyteller can create a sense of instant community among listeners as well as a deep connection with the material being explored (Hamilton and Weiss 2005). Because the storyteller interacts with the audience as the story is told, listeners often feel they become part of the story world. They can even feel as if they are cocreators of the story when it is interactive, when connections with characters are developed, and when empathy is established. Scharner (2019) notes, "We are wired for stories. It's how our brain prefers to receive information" (para. 2). If you've ever heard a good storyteller tell a compelling story, you know it can transport you to another time and place.

In the strategies that follow, students benefit both from listening to stories and from becoming storytellers themselves. As listeners, students are supported in their visualization of the stories, which makes a narrative easier to both imagine and remember (Donovan and Pascale 2022). As storytellers, students develop additional skills, including skilled use of voice, improved verbal and nonverbal communication skills, and sense of pacing. Once stories are developed, you also can ask students to write them down, further enhancing their literacy skills.

When students become storytellers, they fine-tune their communication skills. Oral fluency is developed as students explore vocal tone and inflection, pacing, sound effects, and the addition of rich sensory details to the telling. Listeners feel invited on a journey. Also, participating in the creation and telling of stories brings forward students' voices and their ideas.

Scientific ideas are easily embedded in or teased out of stories. Students find that stories provide vivid contexts that show the relevance and use of scientific thinking. Well-placed scientific problems can easily be connected to characters' dilemmas, requiring solutions in order for the story to advance. Such dilemmas can provide additional points of interaction for students and heighten the dramatic tension of the story.

"The benefits [of storytelling] are enormous. These can include increased enthusiasm for reading, focused engagement and improved listening skills, as well as the development of creative thinking and imagination" (Panckridge 2020, 44). As students create, tell, and retell stories, they also gain fluency in their communication skills, use of descriptive language, and persuasive abilities. They also expand their willingness to revisit, revise, and polish their work. By placing science concepts in story settings, we provide a context that gives further meaning to scientific ideas and adds interest to the stories.

Elements of Storytelling

There are five key elements to storytelling (National Storytelling Network, n.d.). To learn more about these elements, visit **storynet.org/ what-is-storytelling/**.

- **Interaction:** The storyteller actively engages the audience and adapts based on the energy and response of the audience. As a result, every time the story is told it changes.

- **Words:** The storyteller uses words (spoken, signed, or manual) to create connections and invite listeners into the story world through sensory details.

- **Actions:** The story is activated through vocalization, physical movement, and small and large gestures.

Storytelling *(cont.)*

- **Story:** The storyteller shares a narrative that has characters and action.
- **Imagination:** Storytellers encourage the active imagination of the listeners.

Strategies for Storytelling

Prompt

Students are invited to become storytellers themselves as they brainstorm, develop, and perform stories from a given prompt. Using a prompt to support storytelling works to develop many skills—understanding of beginning, middle, and end; character development; and the significance of circumstance, setting, and mood in creating compelling stories that are performed and engage the listener. In this strategy, an interview is used as a prompt. Students conduct an interview as a starting point and then weave a story, using what they learned. Students are charged with finding a way for the story to unfold and are in control of its progression.

Personification

Some people describe assigning human qualities to inanimate objects or ideas as *personification* and assigning human qualities to animals as *anthropomorphism*. Other folks use these terms interchangeably. We will use *personification* to refer to all such assignments of human characteristics, as it is most familiar to teachers and students. However, you should feel free to use what best fits your curriculum. Personification is an ancient storytelling tool that continues today; think of both Aesop and the *Toy Story* movies (Cahill 2006). Stories that give animals and objects human traits allow listeners to think about their shortcomings in a safe way and invite us to think about moral or ethical values. When students personify elements of the natural world such as the sun in a nonfiction narrative, they explore nonfiction concepts from multiple perspectives. These tales engage learners and allow us to consider different perspectives. Because animals and objects take on human characteristics, the strategy also lends itself to figurative language.

> "I cannot emphasize enough the importance of a pause. Placed at strategic moments of the oral storytelling, a pause can enrapture the audience and make them eager to find out what happens next."
>
> —Srividhya Venkat (2020)

Points of Entry

Entering at different points of the story can provide different structures for building a narrative. For example, we can create a prequel that starts before stories, we can add a new segment to the middle of a story, and we sometimes work backward to figure out where we need to begin. These different points of entry provide a frame that can support students' abilities to create a story as well as to gain a deeper understanding of cause-and-effect relationships. In creating such stories, students analyze, evaluate, and create, the three highest-order thinking skills in Bloom's revised taxonomy (Anderson et al. 2000).

Retelling

Storytelling is an oral tradition that is grounded in telling and retelling stories. With each retelling, a story grows more polished and more dramatic, with clear high points and striking moments. Students become more responsive to working with listeners and more adept at using the storytelling process to spark the imagination of the audience. This revisiting of stories also strengthens students' writing skills, as stories get honed and more richly detailed with each retelling.

Students can use the plot of a story as a flexible frame, improvising as the story unfolds. This builds comprehension skills and gives students

Storytelling (cont.)

the opportunity to feel free to adapt the stories based on the response of listeners, dwelling longer on a particular moment or adding embellishment when needed. This responsiveness heightens awareness of the role of an audience, which translates into writing.

Collaborative Storytelling

Collaborative storytelling often takes place in kids' play (Hourcade et al. 2004) and has long been part of the cultural traditions of many families and communities (Coulter, Michael, and Poynor 2007). Students work together to build a story by adding short segments in their oral telling. Stories can be sparked by graphics, character traits, or settings. The story can be "passed" back and forth, with each teller adding details and information before passing it on to the next teller. A natural part of the process is a series of twists and turns that challenge students to maintain a shared story strand, keeping a clear logic so that the story remains together as it unfolds. This challenges them to listen attentively to the details and choices so that they can build on the unfolding events in meaningful and compelling ways by pivoting off given details, such as character traits, circumstances, and action. Students introduce obstacles and innovative solutions that take the characters on surprising journeys. Yew notes that constructing knowledge through the collective creation of narratives can provide more effective ways of learning in group settings than learning concepts individually (2005).

Prompt

Model Lesson: Invent a Scientist

Overview

Students gather primary source information as they interview scientists to find out what they do, what teams they work with, and what problems they have solved with their teams. Students use these problems as prompts to create and tell a story about an imaginary team of scientists solving a scientific problem. Students share their ideas about what a scientist is, use inquiry and research strategies to find out what scientists do, and use their imaginations to create a story in which the characters solve a scientific problem as a team.

Materials

- images of scientists
- *Scientist Interview* (page 32)
- *Story Planning Questions* (page 33)
- *Elements of Storytelling* (page 25)

Standards

Grades K–2

- Knows that asking questions, making observations, and gathering information are ways students can do science
- Shares data with team members or others working on the same problem
- Identifies ways in which voice and sounds may be used to retell a story

Grades 3–5

- Makes observations of construction in the community to make a contribution to science and technology
- Understands that most scientists and engineers work in teams to apply scientific ideas to design, test, and refine their work
- Imagines how a character's inner thoughts impact the story and given circumstances

Grades 6–8

- Makes observations and measurements to engage in any field of science
- Applies scientific ideas to design, test, and refine a device in various settings in which scientists and engineers may work
- Develops a character by articulating the character's inner thoughts, objectives, and motivations

Grades 9–12

- Designs a solution to a complex real-world problem by breaking it down into smaller, more manageable problems
- Uses personal experiences and knowledge to develop a character who is believable and authentic

Prompt (cont.)

Preparation

Locate local or accessible scientists in your community, in your networks, or on the internet. You can find and make connections to scientists by searching "find a scientist" online. The NISE Network (**nisenet.org**) can connect you with nanoscientists in your area who are interested in collaborating with schools and serving as content advisors. Additionally, the Philadelphia Science Festival website (**www.philasciencefestival.org**) has a feature where both scientists and teachers can sign up to connect. You also can contact nearby universities, and, most important, you can ask students and others in your community if they know of any scientists who would serve as resources for the work required of students in this lesson.

Gather a variety of images of scientists to share with students. These images will serve as the foundation for a conversation about who scientists are and what they do. Additional suggestions are provided in the Specific Grade-Level Ideas.

Procedure

1. Ask students what they know about scientists, asking questions such as, "What is a scientist? What stories or movies about scientists have you read and seen? What scientists do you know?" Share images of scientists in a variety of settings and continue to expand on your questions, asking, "Who is a scientist? Where do scientists work and what do they do? What kinds of teams do they work with?" Brainstorm and record a list of as many kinds of scientists as you and your students can think of.

2. Tell students that they will interview scientists about the work they do. Ask them how you as a class can find scientists to interview. Take their suggestions and be sure to add your own if students do not include all viable resources.

3. Place students into small groups and have each group identify a scientist to research. Tell them they can do some research on the internet, but they need to also interview their scientist in person, on the phone, or in a video meeting.

4. Distribute the *Scientist Interview* activity sheet to each student group. For practice, ask students to think about a time when they solved a problem with a team. Have them interview one another about their experience. Ask them to record their data and share with the class what they learned about their interview partner.

5. With your assistance or independently, depending on your students' age and access, have students contact their scientist and conduct an interview. If the scientist is local, students could invite them to class to meet in person. Otherwise, students can conduct their interviews online or over the phone.

6. Have students share their data with the class. Ask questions such as "What kinds of problems did you learn about? Where do your scientists do their work? Who else is involved in the work?"

7. Tell students that they will use what they learned from the interviews to create a story about an imaginary team of scientists solving a problem. Ask each student to think of a scientific problem they want their story to be about. This will be the prompt on which they will base their story. Share the *Elements of Storytelling* and review with the students. Then have students identify a particular issue that the scientist had to wrestle with and how that person worked to resolve it.

Prompt (cont.)

8. Distribute the *Story Planning Questions* activity sheet and direct students to answer the questions and use their answers to develop a story about their imaginary team of scientists. Remind students to use voice and gesture to personify each scientist on the team.

9. Provide time for students to work on their stories and practice telling them aloud to partners or small groups. They should use peer feedback to improve their stories and storytelling.

10. Have students share their final stories with the whole class. Use the Discussion Questions to review and debrief.

Discussion Questions

▸ What did you need to know about science, scientists, and storytelling to develop a believable story?

▸ How did you decide what kind of scientists would be part of your team?

▸ How did you translate your research into the elements of a story, including narrative, actions, movement, words, and character?

▸ How did you make your story interactive for your listeners?

▸ How did telling your story support your understanding of what scientists do?

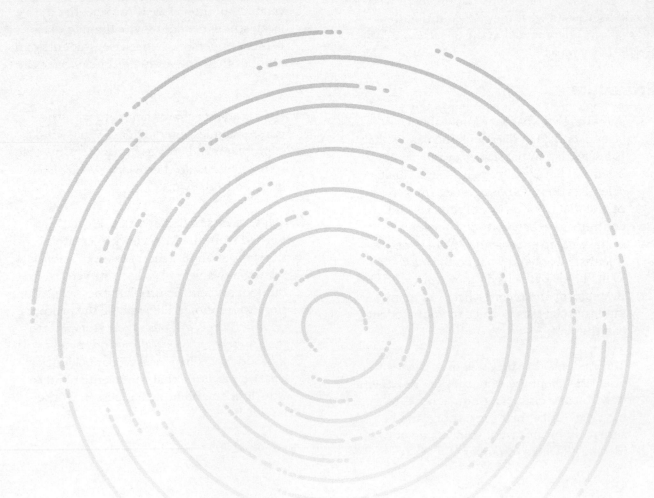

Prompt (cont.)

Specific Grade-Level Ideas

Grades K–2

Invite one or more scientists to visit your classroom. Prepare interview questions by brainstorming with students. What would they like to know about the scientist's work and those they work with? Have students practice asking questions of you or another adult to practice how they will act when the scientist comes. You also could use the questions students brainstormed to interview scientists online.

As a class, talk about the kinds of problems scientists solve with help from others. Then use that information to develop a story together.

Grades 3–5

Have students look at construction in your community (new tunnels, a new museum, a building under restoration) and create a story about a team of people working on the project. Students can explore local issues that require a team of experts from different disciplines to solve a problem (engineers, architects, scientists, and so on).

This strategy can be used to explore any science content by having students investigate and create stories about particular types of scientists and problems scientists solve, ranging from engineering to environmental science to astronomy or medicine.

Grades 6–8

Have each group of students define a local problem and create a story about potential solutions, describing the team and the constraints that they would have to keep in mind when deciding on the solution. Be sure to also include an interesting contingency the team must overcome as they solve the problem. This will provide excitement in the development of the plot.

This strategy can be used to explore any number of problems in multiple areas of science and engineering, as students can investigate local problems in health care, transportation, the environment, or any other scientific topic reflected in their local area.

Grades 9–12

Have students read about a current event in science and bring it to life through storytelling. For example, gather a collection of videos, books, podcasts, and so on around oceanic currents and the movement of trash. Have students create a story about the potential solutions, describing the team and the constraints that they would have to keep in mind when deciding on the solution.

This strategy also can be used to tell the story of a current problem in science from the perspective of a scientist who is wrestling with it.

Scientist Interview

Directions: Use the questions to interview a scientist. Be sure to read the questions in advance. Add any additional questions that seem relevant to your research.

1. What is your name? _____

2. What kind of research and work do you do? What kinds of problems do you work with?

   _____

   _____

3. What skills and habits do you need to have for your work?

   _____

   _____

4. Can you share a scientific problem you solved as a member of a team?

   _____

   _____

5. Can you tell me who made up the team? What skills did each team member bring?

   _____

   _____

6. How did you resolve the problem?

   _____

   _____

7. How did your team share its findings?

   _____

Name: _____ Date: _____

Story Planning Questions

Directions: Answer the questions about your imaginary team of scientists. Use your answers to develop and tell a story.

1. What problem will your team of scientists encounter?

   _____

2. Who are the team members? How will they use their skills to help solve the problem?

   _____

3. How will the team solve the problem?

   _____

4. How will the team share its findings?

   _____

5. How will you create a story with a clear beginning, middle, and end?

   _____

   _____

6. How will you establish your character (personality, way of speaking, and so on)?

   _____

   _____

7. How will you use your words and actions to bring your story to life?

   _____

   _____

8. What story moments will be interactive and how?

   _____

   _____

Personification

Model Lesson: Keystone Species

Overview

In this strategy, students investigate the interconnected relationship of various animals to a keystone species as they tell a story from an animal's point of view (anthropomorphism). Students also could take the perspective of something else in the environment and explore the interconnected relationship from that perspective. Personification and anthropomorphism challenge students to consider new perspectives and explore difficult ethical and moral dilemmas.

Materials

- a book that outlines the life of a particular species and its place in an ecosystem
- *Sample Concept Map* (page 38)
- *Fact Finding and Observations* (page 39)
- *Story Planner* (page 40)
- *Elements of Storytelling* (page 25)

Standards

Grades K–2

- Describes particular environments where some plants and animals can survive well, some survive less well, and some cannot survive at all
- Uses voice and movement in a guided drama experience

Grades 3–5

- Makes a claim that when the environment changes, the types of plants and animals that live there may change
- Investigates how movement and voice are incorporated in a drama work

Grades 6–8

- Analyzes and interprets data to provide evidence for the effects of resource availability on the number of organisms in an ecosystem
- Uses various character objectives in a drama work

Grades 9–12

- Designs, evaluates, and refines a solution for reducing the impacts of human activities on the environment and biodiversity
- Uses personal experiences and knowledge to develop a character who is believable and authentic

    © Shell Education

Personification (cont.)

Preparation

Select a book that outlines the life of a particular species and its place in an ecosystem, such as *At Home with the Gopher Tortoise: The Story of a Keystone Species* by Madeleine Dunphy, or select other similar stories about symbiotic relationships within an ecosystem. Practice reading the book aloud, and as you read, think about how to personify each animal. Experiment with the animals' voices and gestures to make the story come alive. As you read the story, note the different relationships between animals and take note of the interdependence of species and how the balance of an ecosystem can be disrupted by the removal of a single species. Make a list of all the organisms in the ecosystem and decide how the animal names will be distributed to students. Additional suggestions are provided in the Specific Grade-Level Ideas.

Procedure

1. Begin a conversation with students about interdependent relationships by asking questions such as "What do humans need to survive? What do animals need? What would an animal's habitat include? How are animals dependent on other animals or plants?" If students overlook the basic survival needs, be sure to mention water, space, food sources, and shelter.

2. Assign animals from your selected story to students to personify. You may need to assign the same animal to more than one student. Distribute the *Fact Finding and Observations* activity sheet for students to complete as you read the story aloud.

3. Read aloud your selected story about different types of independent relationships. Engage students as data collectors by asking them to listen for their assigned animals in the story and record characteristics of the animals (behavior, physical features, and so on) and how their animal relates to other organisms on the *Fact Finding and Observations* activity sheet. Stop reading occasionally to ask students to point out some of the relationships, such as which animals provide shelter or food for other animals. Ask students what makes a good story. Then, list story elements such as *character, setting, conflict, dialogue,* and *action* for students to reference throughout the lesson.

4. Ask students to discuss how the various species share interdependent relationships. Record students' observations in a concept map. Reference the *Sample Concept Map* as a guide to create one using the students' ideas. Display the class-created map for students to reference throughout the lesson.

5. After each student has shared how their species is connected to the web of relationships, present students with a scenario in which the keystone species is removed from the web. Discuss what would happen and which relationships would be affected both directly and indirectly.

6. Share the *Elements of Storytelling* and review with the students. Group students together who have the same assigned animal and distribute one *Story Planner* activity sheet per group. Direct students to use the chart to help them plan a story about how the disappearance of the keystone species changes their relationships. Ask students to consider the point of view of their animals, and remind them to refer to the concept map. Ask students to create sounds and gestures to personify their animals, such as a rabbit hopping about, a warbler flapping its wings, or a snake slithering along the ground. Circulate as students work, and use the Planning Questions to guide them in developing their stories and characters.

Personification *(cont.)*

7. Have each group of students tell their story to the class to make clear how a wide range of animals can be affected by a single species and how their lives and needs are intertwined. Use the Discussion Questions to debrief. Emphasize how the concept map you recorded as a class helped them remember the information.

Planning Questions

▸ What character traits will your animal have?

▸ Describe the issue that the animal is faced with as a result of the missing animal and how it will deal with it.

▸ What choices does the animal have in dealing with the issue?

▸ What props and gestures can you use to develop your character?

▸ Where will your story unfold?

▸ What will you see, smell, hear, and touch in this setting?

▸ What issue does your animal encounter? What choices does the animal have in dealing with this challenge?

▸ How will you create empathy with your character?

Discussion Questions

▸ How did you create a vivid character?

▸ How did the concept map we recorded as a class help you remember the information in the story?

▸ What are examples of other interdependent relationships?

▸ How did you use the interdependent relationships to help you develop your story?

▸ How did personifying an animal as it coped with the removal of a keystone species help you think about human relationships to animals and their environment?

▸ What story elements did you use to bring your story to life (narrative, actions, movement, and words)?

"To achieve integration of ideas requires making the less visible (molecules, electrons, cell components) and abstract ideas (energy, photosynthesis, entropy) comprehensible to students without obstructions embodied in the symbolic and sometimes obtuse language of science used to communicate these ideas. . . . This is why science teachers often use metaphors and analogies to help students access ideas, explanations and theory."

—Peter J. Aubusson, Allan G. Harrison, and Stephen Ritchie (2006, as cited in Braund and Reiss, 2019, para. 42)

Personification (cont.)

Specific Grade-Level Ideas

Grades K–2

Instead of assigning the names of species for students to personify, distribute pictures of the animals. (*At Home with the Gopher Tortoise: The Story of a Keystone Species* provides great pictures in the back of the book.) Have students tell improvised stories, focusing on the personification of animals in their environments and their need to find food and shelter within a habitat.

Students also could personify a seed as it grows into a plant, an object as it moves across different surfaces, or an object as it spins or rocks back and forth.

Tell a story and invite students to portray the personified characters through movement. Then challenge students to become the storyteller and have the listeners pantomime the action.

Grades 3–5

Draw a concept map of the storytelling experience, encouraging students to improvise and add twists and turns to their story. Students could add interdependent connections to the story that they research independently. Encourage students to recognize the interdependence within food webs and discuss the connections. Be sure to have students consider the point of view of the animal they personify. What is the human impact on their character?

Students also could personify part of a machine that has been lost or the potential uses of a tool.

In addition to narrating a story invite students to create moments of dialogue and interaction between characters.

Grades 6–8

Students can investigate species external to the web in the story. Each student can become a character in the story and create tension and suspense on the existing relationships within the ecosystem. Encourage students to invent character behaviors based on their observations and the emotional responses of their classmates. Investigate animals that students are familiar with that live in local ecosystems (schoolyard, watershed, forest). Discuss the connections between different interdependent relationship cycles. As students personify each animal, ask them to consider the animal's point of view. How does their character view humans? How do humans affect their character and its environment? Invite students to activate the thoughts of a character sharing what's on their mind as part of relaying the story.

Students can personify a molecule of water as it travels through an environment or changes from one state to another (gas to liquid), or they can personify a fossil as it is formed.

Grades 9–12

In addition to the suggestions for grades 6–8, students can personify concepts of astronomy such as a black hole, chemistry concepts of acids and bases, or layers of the atmosphere.

Invite students to integrate the listeners into the story for "choose your own adventure" type tales, where the story can pivot based on feedback from the listeners.

Sample Concept Map

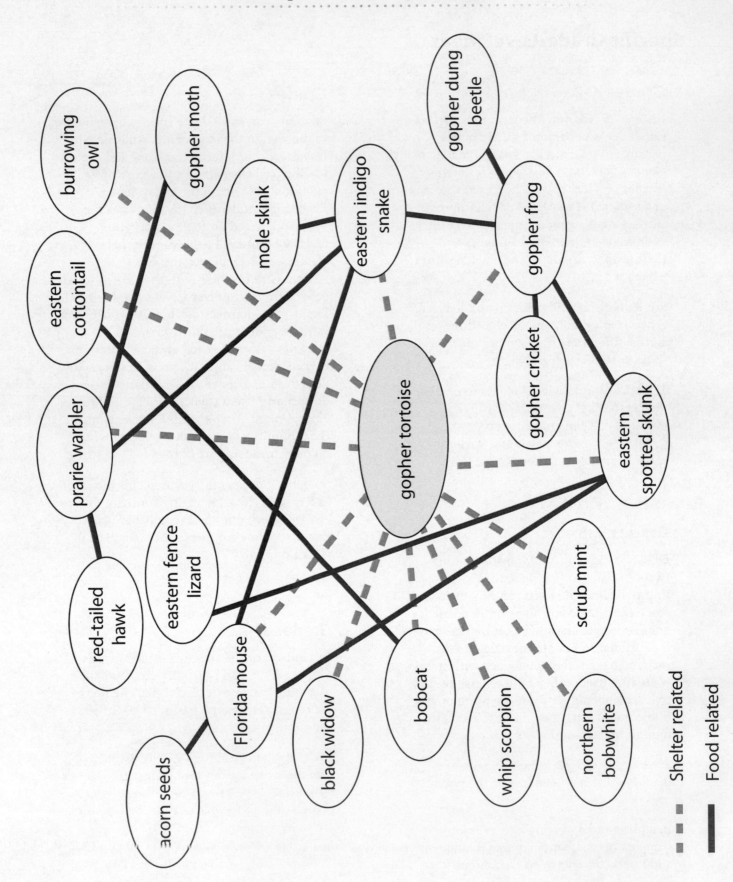

Shelter related

Food related

Name: _____ Date: _____

Fact Finding and Observations

Directions: As you listen to the story, fill in the chart to record information about your animal that will help you create a story.

Animal	
Animal Characteristics	
Habitat (food, shelter, water, space)	
Interdependent Relationships	Animal 1
	Animal 2
	Animal 3

Name: _____ Date:_____

Story Planner

Directions: Use this chart to plan your story.

Storytelling Technique
Personification: How will you personify your animal? List its character traits. How will you use voice and gesture to show these traits?

Story Elements
Beginning: Introduce your animal. Describe the animal in its original habitat, including the location, sounds, water, food, and shelter.
Middle: Describe how and why the keystone species was removed. What is your animal's reaction? What actions does your animal take? What might it be thinking? What might your animal say to communicate its reaction?
End: Describe how your animal survives. Who or what helps it? How does your animal feel? Where does it go? How might you end the story—with a resolution? With a question?

Points of Entry

Model Lesson: Seed Journey Story Enders

Overview

This strategy can be used at any point in a story. In this lesson, students enter a story at the end and work backward. They begin with a plant taking root and work backward to weave a tale about the journey of the seed from its parent plant to its final destination. Students observe seeds closely and conduct research as they develop their seed characters. Developing their story also brings forth the interconnectedness of living things and the distinct characteristics of ecosystems as seeds disperse and grow, encountering forces beyond their control that can take them to new places.

Materials

- assorted seeds
- book about seeds and how they propagate
- *Seed Character Development* (page 46)
- magnifying glasses (*optional*)
- large paper for storyboards
- *Storyboard Planner* (page 47)
- *Storytelling Craft Tips* (page 45)
- *Elements of Storytelling* (page 25)

Standards

Grades K–2

- Describes habitats where some organisms survive well, some survive less well, and some cannot survive at all
- Develops models to describe that organisms go through a process of growth and change
- Contributes to the adaptation of the plot
- Uses and adapts sounds and movements

Grades 3–5

- Constructs an argument with evidence that in a particular habitat an organism's behavior is related to the kinds of organisms present
- Develops models to describe that organisms have unique and diverse life cycles related to their environments
- Revises and improves an improvised or scripted drama work
- Investigates how movement and voice are incorporated into a drama work

Grades 6–8

- Constructs an argument supported by empirical evidence that in an ecosystem relationships are competitive
- Articulates and examines choices to refine a scripted drama work
- Develops effective physical and vocal traits of characters in a drama work

Grades 9–12

- Evaluates evidence for the role of group behavior on individuals' and species' chances to survive and reproduce
- Cooperates as a creative team to make interpretive choices
- Shapes character choices using given circumstances

Points of Entry (cont.)

Preparation

Gather various seeds from your local environment or home and ask students to do the same. Seeds should be easily accessible in a market or the local surroundings (popcorn, dandelion, and the like). Display seeds in the classroom and select one seed, such as a dandelion seed, to develop a sample story with students. Locate an image of the ecosystem in which your chosen seed grows. Select a book about seeds and how they propagate. *Seeds* by Ken Robbins is an excellent resource for inspiration. Additional suggestions are provided in the Specific Grade-Level Ideas.

Procedure

1. Challenge students to identify seeds they know, including the ones they brought from home. Ask them to share what they already know about seeds. Discuss how seeds grow and travel, who or what might help them travel, how far they travel, and by what methods they can travel. Ask students how they could find information about dispersal of particular seeds and their respective habitats. Read aloud a book about seeds, and ask students to imagine that they are one of the seeds.

2. Share the seed you selected, such as a dandelion seed, and an image of the ecosystem in which it grows, such as a school sports field. Ask students to imagine that they are that seed and tell the story of the seed's journey, starting with the end and working backward. Have students consider the following questions: "How did the seed arrive in that field—by a human, by an animal, or by the wind? Where did it come from?" Trace as many steps back as you can until you arrive at the seed separating from its parent plant. As students offer their ideas, record the events of the story and display them so that students can refer to them throughout the lesson.

3. Once the full story is recorded, add details and read the story aloud from the seed's perspective, or invite students to tell the story from the seed's perspective.

4. Have students observe the collection of seeds in the display area and classify them based on how they disperse (by wind, by water, by animals, and so on). If necessary, have students use reference materials to determine this information.

5. Divide the class into small groups and have each group choose a seed from the class collection to research and write a story about. Try to cover all seed dispersal methods among the groups of students. Provide each group with an image of the ecosystem in which their seed grows to use as the end of their story or have students select an image.

6. Distribute the *Seed Character Development* activity sheet. Have students closely observe their seed (use magnifying glasses when appropriate) and research the plant it came from to figure out what conditions it needs to grow and develop. Students also should research the seed's anatomy, method of release or travel, and special conditions for propagation, such as fire or animal digestion. Direct students to gather and document their research on the *Seed Character Development* activity sheet.

7. Remind students of the story they created together at the beginning of this activity. Explain that their groups will write a similar adventure story that tells of their seed's life journey. Share the *Elements of Storytelling* and discuss with students. Invite students to consider the elements as they plan for their storytelling. Tell students their story should be told from the seed's perspective. Challenge them to include information they found in their research.

Points of Entry (cont.)

Ask students how they can bring their story to life in a sensory way. Explain that they should begin their story at the end of the seed's journey and work backward to create the full story. Then, they will retell the story from beginning to end.

8. Distribute a large sheet of paper to each group and have them fold it twice to create four sections to use as a storyboard. Distribute the *Storyboard Planner* activity sheet to help them develop their storyboard. Remind students to begin filling in the *Storyboard Planner* at the end and work backward.

9. Distribute the *Sample Storytelling Techniques* activity sheet. Have students practice telling their stories with other groups, using various voices and intonations to express emotion.

10. Invite groups to share their stories with the whole class. Use the Discussion Questions to review and articulate the connections between science and storytelling.

> "Adding 'theatrical' techniques can make reading more enjoyable for good readers and struggling readers alike."
>
> —Bruce Lansky (2015)

Discussion Questions

▸ What did you learn about your seed through the development of your character?

▸ What impact did the environment have on your seed character?

▸ How did the relationships in your seed's habitat support the plot in your story?

▸ What decisions did you need to make in the creation of your story, and how were these decisions informed by your research?

▸ What story elements did you use as you shared the experience of your character?

Points of Entry (cont.)

Specific Grade-Level Ideas

Grades K–2

The Tiny Seed by Eric Carle is a great resource for students, as it provides a model of a story that tracks a seed's trajectory. This strategy invites students to refine their intuitive understanding of *living* versus *nonliving* and explore and articulate how seeds grow, develop, and reproduce. Students' research will be observational as they notice, make sense of, and articulate what they see. Invite students to tell the story of their seeds closely following the text but adding commentary and movement for their character. Have them create moments of interaction with those listening to the story. This strategy can be used to investigate the life cycle of any living creature or natural phenomenon, such as the water cycle.

Grades 3–5

Have students collect rocks at home and in their local environment, classify them based on particular characteristics, use magnifying glasses to observe details, and research the type of rock and how it's formed. Then have them tell a story that follows the formation of the rock type. Invite students to show the transformation in their bodies as they tell the story. This strategy also can be used to have students explore other living or nonlivings things where transformation is easily observable and can translate into a story with multiple points of entry, such as butterflies or frogs.

Grades 6–8

Have students use points of entry to explain patterns of interactions among organisms, such as competitive, predatory, and mutually beneficial interactions. Students can use this knowledge to build compelling settings for their stories. Have students consider the following: What effect does the organism have on its habitat and vice versa? What competitive and beneficial relationships exist between the organism and other organisms in its environment? How are these relationships visible in the story plot and the interactions between characters? Invite students to make these relationships visible through interaction between the characters such as dialogue and action.

Grades 9–12

Have students conduct investigations around the laws of gravity. They can tell a story that explains the law(s) of gravity they investigated and its importance in the real world. Invite students to bring in different character perspectives to explore the laws of gravity, and include a conflict the characters need to navigate to add dramatic interest.

Name: _____ Date: _____

Storytelling Craft Tips

Find ways to engage the audience. Invite the audience into the story by posing a question.

Repeat lines to heighten audience awareness and add dramatic interest.

Allow your voice to hold emotion, reflecting the intensity of what is happening in the story as it unfolds.

Use facial expressions and eye contact to allow the audience to feel as though they are connected to the story.

Alter the tempo of your speech. Slowing down and speeding up language can intensify the story as the audience is brought along with the pace.

Use descriptive details to help the audience picture the story as it is being told.

Seed Character Development

Directions: Answer the questions to record information about your seed character. You can draw, write, or do both.

What kind of seed are you? What do you look like?
What personality traits do you have?
How do you travel?
Where do you grow?
What kind of conditions do you require?

Name: _____ Date: _____

Storyboard Planner

Directions: Imagine you are a seed. Use the planner to help tell your life story. Start at the end and work backward. Then, tell the story from beginning to end.

Beginning: Time and Place	**Middle: Dangerous Opportunity**
You are in your original habitat with your parent plant. What is your name? How do you feel? What is your habitat like? What sounds can you hear? What is the temperature? Who else is there? _____ _____ _____ _____	*You separate from your parent plant.* How do you separate? What do you notice? Where do you go? What happens? Is there anyone or anything else involved in your separation? _____ _____ _____ _____
Middle: Seed Journey	**End: Arrival and Transformation**
You are traveling to your new home. Where do you go? How do you travel? Who or what helps you along? How does that make you feel? What challenges do you encounter? How do you overcome them? _____ _____ _____ _____	*You arrive at your destination.* What beneficial or competitive forces exist here? How does this place transform you? How do you feel here? What does this place look like? Feel like? Sound like? Who else is here? _____ _____ _____ _____

Retelling

Model Lesson: Folktales and Sustainable Agriculture

Overview

In this lesson, students investigate a traditional folktale that reflects how different cultures use biodiversity in agriculture. Students investigate the scientific principles identified in the folktale and determine the most important aspects to retell, while adding their own interpretation and language to integrate scientific explanations reflected in the folktale.

Materials

- collection of different versions of the folktale "The Three Sisters"
- index cards
- *Retelling Plan* (page 52)
- *Elements of Storytelling* (page 25)

Standards

Grades K–2

- Develops a model using an example to describe how Earth's materials consist of solid rocks, soils, liquid water, and the gases of the atmosphere
- Reads folktales appropriate to grades K–2
- Adapts voice level, phrasing, and intonation for different situations

Grades 3–5

- Makes a claim that when the environment changes, the types of plants and animals that live there may change
- Uses physical and vocal exploration for character development

Grades 6–8

- Constructs a scientific explanation based on evidence in which organisms interact and depend on one another in an ecosystem
- Identifies and develops effective physical and vocal traits of a character

Grades 9–12

- Obtains and combines information about ways human activities have had major effects on the land, vegetation, streams, ocean, air, and even outer space
- Applies scientific principles to design a method for monitoring human activities that have destroyed natural habitats and caused the extinction of other species
- Explores physical, vocal, and physiological choices to develop a performance that is believable and authentic

Retelling (cont.)

Preparation

The American Indian story "The Three Sisters" is about corn, squash, and beans that grow together and support one another. The corn serves as a stalk for the beans to hold on to, and the squash crawls underneath, providing shade to prevent weeds from growing. The beans in turn support the fertility of the soil. This practice of intercropping is widely used in organic agriculture. There are other folktales from other cultures that include this same concept.

Conduct an internet search for different versions of the legend of "The Three Sisters," or select a folktale that similarly discusses gardening, collaboration, nutrition, and agriculture.

Select multiple versions of the tale to share with students and practice reading them aloud. Pick four events from the story and write them on four separate index cards. These will serve as cues for you to remember the storyline as you tell it to students. Practice telling the story using your four cue cards.

Review the principles of organic agriculture. A great online source is the International Federation of Organic Agriculture Movements (**www.ifoam.org**). This website has a wide range of information about organic agriculture and its impact on the environment. Think of ways in which the folktale includes traditional practices that are now accepted as scientifically sustainable practices. Additional suggestions are provided in the Specific Grade-Level Ideas.

Procedure

1. Introduce oral storytelling to students by explaining that stories are told and retold across cultures for a variety of reasons: to entertain, to educate, to preserve history, to share tradition, to question, and to explain phenomena. Discuss with students how folktales have been told and retold over time and how stories have been passed orally from generation to generation. Ask students, "Do you think the details of the story stay the same each time they are retold, or do they change? Why?" Ask students what makes a compelling story. Share *Elements of Storytelling* and discuss with students. Invite students to consider the elements as they plan for their storytelling. How might they adjust the way story elements are used to enhance the telling and engage the audience to feel as if they are part of the story? Ask them to think of stories they have heard more than once in their homes, communities, or classrooms, and ask them to consider how those stories change with each retelling.

2. Tell students that they are going to experience storytelling through the oral tradition. The story elements will stay the same, but the details will evolve with each retelling. Explain that they will investigate a traditional American Indian folktale that represents contemporary agricultural practices.

3. Tell the story of "The Three Sisters" to students as practiced, or tell the folktale of your choice and share additional versions. Ask students to keep track of how each variation differs.

4. Ask students to consider what information stays the same in the different versions. Ask students to identify the scientific content in the tales and whether or not this information changes. Discuss with students what scientific processes are at work. Ask them to name as many scientific processes as they can in relation to the story. Record this information for students to refer to throughout the lesson.

Retelling (cont.)

5. Divide the class into small groups and distribute the *Retelling Plan* activity sheet to each group. Instruct groups to select one version of the story to retell. Have students reread the tale and mark the important parts that they will include in their retelling. Ask them also to mark the places where they can connect to specific scientific content and where they can bring it to life through storytelling (e.g. a character's realization, a moment of action, a moment of conflict). Then, have them complete the *Retelling Plan* activity sheet.

6. Walk around and monitor groups, reminding students that it is okay to leave out some details but to make sure they include key scientific details using current information. Tell students that in this type of retelling, the story is not fixed but shifts with each retelling. They should capture the essence of the story using their own interpretation.

7. Have groups retell their tale several times with other small groups. Invite students to find ways to bring character personalities to life (e.g. ways of moving or speaking, or rich descriptions in the storytelling).

8. Invite students to share their story with the whole class. Use the Discussion Questions to debrief.

> "Storytelling can be a powerful way to nurture engagement with science."
>
> —Michael F. Dahlstrom (2014)

Discussion Questions

▸ What did you notice about your story as you retold it again and again while integrating new scientific details?

▸ What changed in your retelling? What remained the same?

▸ How did retelling your story affect your ability and confidence as a storyteller? How did it solidify your scientific understanding of the concepts involved?

▸ How were the elements of storytelling used to convey ideas in the story?

▸ Discuss your artistic choices in telling the story.

Specific Grade-Level Ideas

Grades K–2

Read picture books of folktales from various cultures and select one for the class to retell together or in small groups. Students can draw simple pictures to represent the beginning, middle, and end of their story. As they retell, they can refer to the pictures.

This strategy also can be used to retell classic folktales about animals, such as "The Tortoise and the Hare," and to consider how animals have varying characteristics. Emphasize these characteristics by creating signature gestures that represent or amplify these traits to be performed during storytelling. Many children's stories can be retold by integrating ideas about science, such as *The Very Hungry Caterpillar* by Eric Carle. Students can work as a group to tell the story along with what is happening scientifically.

Retelling (cont.)

Specific Grade-Level Ideas (cont.)

Grades 3–5

Encourage students to try different leads as they retell their stories. For example, what would the effect be if they were to begin their oral retelling with a scientific question or by describing the setting? Ask students to consider how the seed or plant characters affect the soil character and how the plants function within the ecosystem to support one another's growth. They can integrate these scientific explanations into their retelling of the story. This strategy also can be used with other kinds of stories to consider how nature works. Consider, for example, folktales and legends about the sun and the moon or about how mountains and lakes were formed. Browse the internet for folktales or legends and add the specific science content you are interested in addressing. For example, if you search for "folktales about water," you will find a wealth of stories from around the world related to water.

Grades 6–8

Gather a collection of folktales from various cultures that include similar examples of symbiotic plants that can benefit each other in a number of different ways. Examples include canopy coverage (shade-grown coffee), nitrogen fixation (beans), pest management (gardening with pest suppressors, such as pepper, or beneficial insects, such as ladybugs), and the way plants are positioned in the landscape. Ask students to include in their retellings information about how the various elements (light, water, soil, plants,

Grades 6–8 (cont.)

humans, and so on) work to the benefit of one another; they can also integrate contemporary scientific understandings. Challenge students to use the elements of storytelling to draw attention to key ideas in science.

Browse the internet for "folktales for middle school" and select stories that focus on the impact of ecosystems on particular characters, such as animals.

Grades 9–12

Have students investigate how farms implement organic growing methods today. Explore how a particular method has changed or been influenced by technology or genetic engineering and how this will impact future generations.

You also can invite students to write an original myth or folktale to respond to a present-day issue and retell the story for others.

Browse the internet for folktales related to any issue students may be interested in. Have them retell these folktales and use technology to record the retellings. Have students note the evolution of their storytelling over time.

Name: _____ Date: _____

Retelling Plan

Directions: As you create a new version of the folktale, work with your group to answer the following questions. Consider how to tell the story in a way that integrates science content and makes it exciting through the use of the elements of storytelling.

What important **narrative threads** do we need to include in our retelling?
What does the **character** want? What are the character's **traits** and **motivations**? How will you communicate this in your storytelling?
What important **scientific concepts** do we need to include in our retelling?
What **narrative details** are worth developing further in our retelling? What action will unfold? What problem will the character need to solve?
What **scientific details** are worth developing further in our retelling?
How will we **introduce** our story?

Collaborative Storytelling

Model Lesson: Investigating Systems

Overview

In this strategy, students develop a story by building on parts of a story offered by other students. Students investigate the systems that work together to provide them with what they need. By tracking back how a glass of water traveled to the classroom, students understand the multiple systems at play and develop a collaborative story about water moving through both natural and engineered systems.

Materials

- objects to serve as "talking sticks"
- *Refining the Story* (page 56)
- drawing supplies (*optional*)
- *Elements of Storytelling* (page 25)

Standards

Grades K–2

- Describes how people depend on various technologies at home and school
- Contributes ideas for dialogue and plot while collaborating on character development
- Uses voice, gesture, and movement to communicate emotions

Grades 3–5

- Identifies scientific discoveries about the natural world that lead to new and improved technologies
- Identifies human needs and wants that a scientific discovery from the natural world fulfilled
- Collaborates to devise original ideas for a drama/theater work
- Makes physical choices to develop a character and create meaning

Grades 6–8

- Identifies engineering advances that have led to important discoveries in virtually every field of science
- Gathers information and describes that synthetic materials come from natural resources and impact society
- Develops an improvised character by considering inner thoughts, objectives, and motivations
- Uses various physical choices and character objectives in collaborative drama/theater work

Grades 9–12

- Evaluates or refines a technological solution that reduces impacts of human activities on natural systems
- Understands the effects of an author's style and complex literary devices and techniques on the overall quality of a work
- Uses a variety of verbal and nonverbal techniques for presentations and demonstrates poise and self-control while presenting

Collaborative Storytelling (cont.)

Preparation

Conduct research about water in the local community and make a list of the multiple systems involved in bringing water into your classroom. This research will help you guide students in tracking the systems that are involved. Additional suggestions are provided in the Specific Grade-Level Ideas.

Procedure

1. Ask students to consider why they need water and discuss their ideas. Show students a glass of water and ask them how the water came to be in that glass. Explain that you poured it from the faucet, but how did it get to the faucet? With students, trace the process as far back as you can, including the pipes, the soil, the rain, and so on. Record all the steps for students to refer to throughout the lesson.

2. Divide the class into groups of 4 or 5, and have students research the various systems that are involved in getting water to homes, businesses, and schools, including both natural and engineered processes. Revisit the steps you recorded as a class in step 1 to revise and add new information according to students' research.

3. Tell students that they will work together to develop a collaborative story about water, using what they know about water delivery systems. Share the *Elements of Storytelling* and discuss with students. Invite students to consider the elements as they plan for their storytelling. Have each group select a "talking stick" to signify whose turn it is to add to the story. This can be any hand-held item, such as a ruler or a pencil.

4. Provide students with a prompt to spark a story that they will tell together. The prompt could be fantastical, such as "An outer space creature keeps inhaling all the moisture from Earth's atmosphere, and as soon as more water evaporates, the creature takes it in." Or the prompt could be more practical, such as "Chemical pollutants have spilled into the creek where local residents get their water."

5. Have students sit with their groups in a circle and hand the talking stick to the first storyteller. This student begins the story by telling a few details. That student should then pass the talking stick on to the next student, who adds additional information before passing the stick on, and so forth. Student groups can decide to pass the talking stick around the circle, or they can raise their hands when they have ideas to contribute.

6. After the story has been told one time through, distribute the *Refining the Story* activity sheet to each group. Ask students to consider the characters, setting, and plot development of their stories, including the moment of crisis, resolution, and ending, and record them on the activity sheet. Then, ask students to add to, refine, or embellish their story and record these ideas as well.

7. Have students practice telling the new, improved version of their story, refining as needed. Ask them to consider who will tell which parts.

8. Have each group tell their story to the class. Use the Discussion Questions to debrief.

"Science is messy, full of plot twists and competing interpretations—and the way we talk about it should reflect that truth."

—Jim Kozubek (2018, para. 1)

Collaborative Storytelling *(cont.)*

Discussion Questions

▸ How did developing the story collaboratively help you listen?

▸ How did you apply your new understanding in the context of the story plot?

▸ How did the character(s) develop as each student added to the story?

▸ How did the process of improvising a story as a group affect your understanding of storytelling, plot, characters, and story development?

Specific Grade-Level Ideas

Grades K–2

Have students focus on basic needs, such as water or food. Have students consider, for example, how an apple gets to homes. Ask questions such as "Who brings it home? How? Where did that person buy it? How did it get to the store? How did it get to the truck that brought it to the store?" Have students tell the story from the point of view of the apple. It may be best to collaboratively tell the story as a whole class sitting in a circle. The story also can be developed into a collaborative storybook by giving each student one part of the story to illustrate. This strategy can be used to investigate systems for any need such as food, water, or clothing. The work can encompass social systems, technological systems such as cars, and natural ecosystems.

Grades 3–5

Have students investigate goods that have been packaged and that may include more than one ingredient. They can research what went into producing that good, the technologies used, the various ingredients from different places, and the costs, both environmental and economic. Invite students to envision their goods as characters, giving them unique names, character traits, and gestures to bring them to life.

Grades 6–8

Students can investigate the costs and benefits of getting something to the market. They can break into groups to investigate the various technologies that go into one product, such as communication, transportation, and agricultural technologies.

Challenge students to use the elements of storytelling to create compelling scenarios that shed light on the relationships between characters representing different technologies.

Grades 9–12

Students can investigate life-cycle assessments that include both energy and material inputs as well as environmental by-products. A great resource for students to understand the process of life-cycle assessment is *Twinkie Deconstructed* by Steve Ettlinger. Students can develop stories in small groups about a particular product or technology and work together to consider how technology can help mitigate or eliminate some of the harmful unintended consequences. Students can create characters that play out the impact of consequences.

Name: _____ Date: _____

Refining the Story

Directions: After your first round of collaborative storytelling, complete the chart with information about your story. Then add details to embellish the story. You can add more obstacles before the resolution or other pieces to make the story more engaging. Then retell your new version of the story.

Story title:
Nature of the problem:
Character(s):
Setting:
Moment of crisis (What happens in the story that creates tension with the characters?):
Resolution (How do the characters manage their way through the moment of crisis?):
Ending (What happens after the crisis is resolved?):

Drama

Drama

Understanding Drama

Integrating drama into the science classroom can deepen students' connection with science concepts and foster students' ability to find relevance to their own lives and interests. Drama can provide engaging contexts for exploring scientific ideas. By enacting scenes that connect to a science concept or skill, students can apply their learning in real-world settings. Drama strategies work well out-of-doors where students can take advantage of space and natural settings.

When we integrate drama into the science classroom, we invite our students to consider particular situations in which scientific ideas are embedded. As students explore these scenarios, they uncover and deepen their scientific thinking, make personal connections to the sciences, and recognize their real-world relevance. Christopher Andersen (2004) notes that drama has the ability to recreate the essential elements in the world; as such, drama can place science in authentic situations that make sense to students.

When students explore science through the lens of a character, they are called upon to imagine themselves working through processes, events, and dilemmas. In their roles they must make choices, solve problems, translate concepts, and articulate ideas. This process requires students to explain, persuade, clarify, and negotiate their thinking (Elliott-Johns et al. 2012). As students investigate perspectives that are different from their own, they expand their worldviews and develop an awareness of their own. Such experiences help students clarify their thinking, understand different perspectives, and consider new strategies for solving problems.

Drama will provide students with contexts that can ground their scientific investigations. And of course, through dramatic explorations, students also learn and develop skills in drama.

Many of these strategies incorporate process drama, in which the teacher and students work together to explore a problem or situation without a script through improvisation (O'Neill 1995). This allows the drama to develop organically, with students' ideas and impulses leading the way. These drama strategies provide a rich context for scientific investigations where students imagine themselves in a variety of science-related situations. Embedding scientific ideas into dramatic scenarios motivates students to participate eagerly in the exploration of ideas from multiple perspectives.

Elements of Drama

In the field of drama there are many different ideas about which elements are important in dramatic work. These definitions are adapted from a variety of sources, including the "Drama Handbook" (International School of Athens, n.d.), "The 12 Dramatic Elements" (Cash, n.d.), and "Elements of Drama" (Windmill Theatre Company, n.d.).

- **Roles:** The characters (people, animals, objects, ideas, and more) in a drama.

- **Tension**: Dramatic friction or opposition that emerges from a conflict, struggle, or juxtaposition of ideas or motivations; dramatic tension drives action and generates interest.

- **Time**: The pacing of how action moves as the drama unfolds.

- **Dialogue**: The words spoken by characters in a drama.

- **Situations**: The circumstances that frame the drama and identify what is happening and what the problem is.

- **Space**: Where the drama unfolds or the use of the performance space; also the positioning of the body across levels in space (low, medium, and high).

Strategies for Drama

Visualization

In this strategy, students imagine a moment as it unfolds by listening to a sensory description read aloud. Sometimes called mental movie, guided imagery, or guided tour, a dramatic visualization invites students into the world of a text, character, moment, or setting. Teachers use this strategy to "build background knowledge and experience, both factual and emotional, about an event and to build interest on a topic or story" (Neelands and Goode, n.d.). There are a variety of ways to use visualization. For example, you can read a text or tell a story using vivid details to portray a character who moves through a scene. Students use visualization to experience the character's perspective and explore the setting with the sights and sensory details as if moving through it themselves. "Ideally the text is in the second person ('you' form) and includes rich sensory detail to engage students more deeply in the situation or a dilemma" (Neelands and Goode, n.d.). This can serve as a prewriting or prereading activity to engage students more deeply with content.

Tableaux

Sometimes called image theater or human sculpture, *tableau* is a French word that means "frozen picture." It is a drama technique that gives students an opportunity to explore an idea without movement or speaking. In this strategy, students use their bodies individually or in small groups to create an image to tell a story, represent a concept literally, or create a tangible representation of an abstract concept. Working with physical stance (low, medium, high), suggested relationships (body placement and eye contact), and a sense of action frozen in time encourages students to explore ideas and provides a range of ways for students to share what they know about a concept. One person can create a frozen image, or a group can work together. The process of creating group tableaux

prompts discussion of the characteristics of what is being portrayed. The learning occurs in the process of translating ideas to physical representation. Tableaux can also be used as a way to gain entry into a complex idea or bigger project (Walker, Tabone, and Weltsek 2011).

Monologue

A *monologue* is a dramatic scene performed by one person. In creating a monologue, students take on the perspective of a character in a story, real or imagined, and speak directly to the audience for one to three minutes. The character must be established without interacting with others (that would be a dialogue) and must speak in a way that engages the audience with this singular focus.

Often there are monologues in stories and plays that illuminate what a character is thinking. Most often, a monologue reveals a conflict of some kind that the character is wrestling with, a choice to be made, or a problem to be solved. Note that variations include soliloquy, in which a character speaks to themselves. The creation of a monologue provides the opportunity to investigate what Barry Lane calls a "thoughtshot" of a character's inner thinking (1992).

This strategy encourages students to "get into the head" of a particular character. Eventually the goal is for students to create their own monologues, but you may want to introduce the strategy by having students explore prepared ones in resources such as *Magnificent Monologues for Kids 2: More Monologues for Every Occasion* by Chambers Stevens and *Minute Monologues for Kids* by Ruth Mae Roddy.

Next, students can develop characters and create and perform monologues for inanimate objects or forces, or they can portray specific characters (a historical figure; a character from a book, a newspaper article, or a painting; or an imagined character they have created). In order

Drama (cont.)

for a monologue to be dramatic, the character must have some tension or conflict that they are wrestling with. This conflict can be an internal or external dilemma. Its resolution or the exploration of this tension creates dramatic interest.

Mantle of the Expert

Developed by dramatist Dorothy Heathcote, this strategy asks students to imagine that they have a particular expertise that informs how they approach their work and how they present their ideas. Inviting students to imagine that they have a specific frame of reference can be a catalyst that deepens their interest and sense of authority in an area of study. Heathcote and Bolton (1995) note, "Thinking from within a situation immediately forces a different kind of thinking. Research has convincingly shown that the determining factor in children's ability to perform particular intellectual tasks is the context in which the task is embedded. In mantle of the expert, problems and challenges arise within a context that makes them both motivating and comprehensible" (viii).

When students are in a dramatic role, they begin to think through the lens of the character they are playing, developing the attitude and ways of thinking of a scientific expert. Being asked questions about the decisions they make in role, called "hot seating," can draw evidence of students' scientific thinking.

Teacher in Role

In process drama, the teacher and students work together to explore a problem or situation in an unscripted manner through improvisation (O'Neill 1995). In this strategy, the teacher takes on the role of a character to introduce a drama. Teachers can model the kind of work they will ask students to do or set the stage for a dramatic scene. Either way, the strategy serves as an invitation for students to join in the dramatic work, to imagine, or to consider *what if?* There are a variety of ways that the teacher can create this role. For example, the teacher can portray a scientist in a book who presents their predictions and research, become a historical figure in engineering who shares thoughts on possible designs that would impact an environmental issue that would have significant impact on future events, or introduce an investigation by depicting a scientist who shares the details of an observation and asks others to participate as related characters. The allure of seeing their teacher willing to engage in the creation of a scene compels students to suspend their disbelief and join in the dramatic enactment.

Visualization

Model Lesson: Life Processes

Overview

In this lesson, the teacher reads a script with rich, sensory details that encourages students to become part of an imagined world within a curriculum area (experiencing it by imagining what they see, hear, feel, taste, and smell as the script is read). Students explore how descriptive words can create a sensory experience, deepening their interest and understanding of a topic.

Materials

▸ *Sample Scenario 1* (page 66)

▸ *Sample Scenario 2* (page 67)

▸ *Elements of Drama* (page 59)

Standards

Grades K–2

▸ Describes how human activities affect the cultural and environmental characteristics of places or regions

▸ Envisions and engages in a guided drama experience

▸ Applies skills and knowledge from other content areas in a guided drama experience

Grades 3–5

▸ Explains how the cultural and environmental characteristics of places change over time

▸ Articulates visual details of imagined worlds while engaging in a drama experience

▸ Applies skills and knowledge from other content areas in a guided drama experience

Grades 6–8

▸ Describes the cycling of matter and flow of energy among living and nonliving parts of an ecosystem

▸ Articulates visual details of imagined worlds while engaging in a drama experience

▸ Applies skills and knowledge from other content areas in a guided drama experience

Grades 9–12

▸ Explains, based on evidence, how factors affect biodiversity and populations in ecosystems of different scales

▸ Constructs mental images (visualization)

▸ Identifies universal themes or common social issues and expresses them through a drama/theater work

Visualization (cont.)

Preparation

Review *Sample Scenario 1* and *Sample Scenario 2*. Select a script and adapt it as needed for students and area of focus. Play with the tone of your voice to communicate emotion and set the stage for the visualization. Your willingness to be dramatic will intrigue students and help them to feel comfortable in taking their own dramatic risks. Additional suggestions are provided in the Specific Grade-Level Ideas.

Procedure

1. Introduce students to the idea of a visualization. Explain that a visualization is a drama strategy that uses voice and imagination to create a sensory scene through the imagination.

2. Invite students to find a comfortable place to relax and step into their imagination. They can close their eyes if it feels comfortable, or they can soften their gaze or lower their eyes, making it easier to focus inwardly.

3. Read the *Sample Scenario* visualization, including any variations or modifications you chose to make to it. Make your voice match the meaning to enhance the sensory experience. Encourage students to "look around in their mind's eye" and notice how imagination sparks their senses.

4. Invite students to share their experiences with visualization, noticing individual and sensory connections and insights. Discuss unique interpretations of the experience.

5. Choose an area of your curriculum and create a visualization together with input from your students. For example, the visualization could be based on a scene from a book and be written in the second person ("you") so that students focus on entering the world of the text. You could draw descriptive material from a book, painting, dance, music, photograph, and so on to serve as a descriptive narration of what is unfolding. Encourage students to use their imagination to include sensory details.

6. Debrief, using the Discussion Questions.

Discussion Questions

▸ Tell me about your imagined experience.

▸ What did you notice (see, feel, taste, hear, smell) as you imagined the text?

▸ What emotions did you experience? Memories?

▸ What insights do you have as a result of this experience?

▸ What connections did you make to the text?

Visualization (cont.)

Specific Grade-Level Ideas

Grades K–2

Invite students to create a visualization to explore weather events. Challenge them to write their visualizations from the perspective of the weather. You might have them imagine patterns and variations in local weather, exploring sunlight, wind, snow, or rain and how temperature in different regions affects the weather. Have students imagine they are one of the following:

▸ a blizzard blowing through the streets of your town or city

▸ a thunderstorm forming, storming, and winding down

▸ springtime rain bringing flowers to life in a field

Invite students to share their visualizations. Discuss how the different weather events were represented in the visualizations and how the sensory details brought the reader/listener in to the moment.

Grades 3–5

Ask students to document their understanding of the effects of erosion from water, ice, wind, or vegetation by writing a visualization from the perspective of one of these natural forces. Have students imagine they are one of the following:

▸ wind eroding the top layer of soil of a field, creating a dust storm

▸ waves reshaping the coast in a winter storm

▸ water carving out canyons over time

Invite students to perform their visualization. Discuss how the visualization engages the reader or listener in experiencing how these forces shape our landscapes through sensory connections.

Visualization (cont.)

Specific Grade-Level Ideas (cont.)

Grades 6–8

Have students explore how substances are made from different types of molecules. Invite students to explore the physical and chemical properties for material in sensory detail. Their visualizations should be written from the perspective of the states of matter—solid, liquid, or gas—describing how they move relative to each other, if they collide, how fast they vibrate and move location, and respond to temperature change.

Invite students to read their visualizations aloud. Discuss what happens at the molecular level as particles combine to produce a substance with different properties and how these ideas were brought to life through visualization.

Grades 9–12

In addition to the suggestions for grades 6–8, have students extend the visualization about the seed to create their own visualization about factors that affect biodiversity and populations in ecosystems of different scales. Instruct students to use text evidence from their own research or other sources within their visualization.

Encourage students to explore an astronaut's account of space travel and exploration and write a visualization sharing the wonder and awe of the universe, including key facts and information about recent historical and upcoming space events. Students also could use their research to create a visualization predicting what might occur in future space exploration.

This strategy also could be used to create visualizations about properties of waves and electromagnetic radiation.

"Humans are visual creatures by nature. People absorb information in graphic form that would elude them in words. Images are effective for all kinds of storytelling, especially when the story is complicated, as it so often is with science. Scientific visuals can be essential for analyzing data, communicating experimental results and even for making surprising discoveries."

—Betsy Mason (2019, para. 2)

Sample Scenario 1

Imagine you are a tiny seed—you are tucked neatly into the head of a colorful orange flower, enjoying the summer sun and gentle breeze. Suddenly the wind picks up and tugs at you . . . you feel yourself pulling free from the flower, and with another gust you are whisked away, higher and higher into the air.

You are carried by the wind over fields and trees and lakes until you land here in this soft field. You fall in deep soil that is damp and warm. Notice how your seed coat protects you from the wet and cold. You are warm and safe. You sleep, exhausted from the travel for what feels like days on end. Then one day you wake, noticing that you feel a sense of warmth coming from above. The sun is rising and warming the soil around you. You feel warm and cozy tucked tightly inside your coat. You hear the sounds of a soft rain pittering and pattering. Pittering and pattering. The water soaks down into the ground. You hear the water trickling down into the soil around you.

Over time you notice that your seed coat is softening as it absorbs the water. It begins to pull away from your body. A small seam opens, and you are exposed to the soil. At first you wonder what is going on, but then you feel it. Something inside you is changing. Something is yearning, stretching. A small root emerges from your base, pushing beyond your seed coat into the soil. It moves more deeply into the soil. It feels soooo good to stretch out and expand. You notice that you are thirsty and hungry, and the tiny root moves deeper down, expanding, allowing you to draw from the rich nutrients in the soil. You hear the sound of a gentle shower above you. The water washes down and surrounds you. You drink deeply.

Each day as you stretch and grow more roots, you take in the soil nutrients and nourishing rain. Your seed coat falls away, and a new shoot emerges, this time traveling up toward the sun. You can feel when your stem bursts through the soil for the first time, free to travel up, up, up toward the sun. Your roots travel down, and out. Your stem travels up and bursts forward with leaves, with buds. And suddenly, your buds explode into flower. You are exuberant. Bees come and drink your nectar. Butterflies flit around you. Life is wonderful. Time goes by, the fall arrives, and your flower petals drop. You bring in your energy and wait for the wind to come, to take your seeds to new places. You smile, sigh, and think . . . *Wait, just wait my children. Your time will come.*

Visualization by Lisa Donovan. Used by permission.

Sample Scenario 2

Imagine you are a honeybee. You are leaving the hive in search of nectar. You fly high above the hive, side-by-side with other workers on a similar mission. The sunlight hits your back and glistens on your wings. You catch the distinct scent of nectar warming in the summer sun, and it leads you to a field of wildflowers waving their colorful blooms to and fro.

You are drawn to a blue flower rich with the scent of sweet nectar. You land lightly on a soft petal, then make your way to the center of the flower. You probe the flower with your tongue, similar to a straw, your proboscis. You lower your tongue down, down, down into the flower. And suddenly it's there: nectar, rich and sweet.

Visualization by Lisa Donovan. Used by permission.

Source of information used for this visualization: "A Closer Look at How Bees Make Honey." www.perfectbee.com.

Tableaux

Model Lesson: Sculpting the Changing Environment

Overview

In this strategy, students create *tableaux*, a French word meaning "frozen pictures," to create a tangible representation of factors that affect the health of a particular environment. By building a sculpture with their bodies, students investigate and represent ways in which humans impact the environment. Working with the placement of one's body on different levels (low, medium, high), relationships (body placement and eye contact), and a sense of action frozen in time gives students the opportunity to explore ideas and provides a range of ways for students to share what they know.

Materials

▸ images that show human impact on the environment

▸ *Tableaux Tips* (page 73)

▸ *Gallery Walk Observation Sheet* (page 74)

▸ *Elements of Drama* (page 59)

Standards

Grades K–2

▸ Makes claims about how environmental changes could affect people's health

▸ Describes solutions to reduce the impact of humans on the land, water, air, and/or other living things

▸ Collaborates to develop a guided drama experience

Grades 3–5

▸ Analyzes the ways people alter the physical environment

▸ Applies scientific principles to design a method for monitoring and minimizing human impact on the environment

▸ Collaborates to develop and present a drama/theater work

Grades 6–8

▸ Applies scientific principles to design a method for monitoring and minimizing human impact on the environment

▸ Explains how human activity and the use of renewable and nonrenewable resources have changed the climate

▸ Demonstrates mutual respect for self and others while incorporating ideas to develop and present a drama/theater work

Grades 9–12

▸ Evaluates the claims, evidence, and reasoning that biological magnification in ecosystems changes conditions and may result in a new ecosystem

▸ Communicates directorial choices for improvised or scripted scenes

Tableaux *(cont.)*

Preparation

Decide the specific content on which students will focus. Find images that students can draw from for information about the impact of humans on the environment, including purposeful changes to landscape, such as irrigation, or unintended consequences, such as deforestation or pollution.

Think about how to group students so that more complex ideas can be represented. Students can be asked to create an individual tableau, work in small groups, or represent more complex ideas best portrayed in larger groups of five or six students. Additional suggestions are provided in the Specific Grade-Level Ideas.

Procedure

1. Introduce students to the particular environmental content on which they will focus. Share images that depict some of these processes, and ask students to discuss what may have happened before each image was taken. Ask: "How might the scene have looked different? What do you think happened? How has it changed?"

2. Introduce what a *tableau* is by inviting two students to join you in front of the class. Tell students that they will create a frozen picture depicting an environmental concept. You can facilitate this by describing how you want them to position their bodies or by modeling for them so that they can mirror what you do. For example, invite one student to stand tall with their arms spread open as if they were the branches of a living tree. Invite the other student to bend at the waist with wilted arms to represent a felled tree. Ask the viewers to identify the illustrated concept.

3. Distribute *Tableaux Tips* and review with the students. To further demonstrate the concept of a tableau, invite five students to the front of the room and suggest that they arrange themselves to form a variety of activities that change our physical environment and the climate. For example, one student could be planting crops in the soil, another could be a builder, and another could be driving a car. Have students talk about the differences between an individual tableau and a group tableau, and the differences between one person directing the composition of the image and using group decision-making.

4. Divide students into groups and assign each group a specific environmental issue to illustrate through creating tableaux. Provide groups with resource materials or have them research images and text to inform their tableaux. Choose from the following grouping options:

   ▸ Have students work in pairs. One student is the "sculptor" and the other is "clay." The sculptor directs the composition of the image with suggestions about ways to position the body using the *Tableaux TIps.*

   ▸ Have students work in small groups. One or two group members go to the center of the room and begin the sculpture with a pose that represents a landscape or environment. The rest of the participants add on, one by one, to create a group sculpture depicting ongoing changes in the environment, until all group members are involved. Suggested terms to explore include *air pollution, deforestation,* and *ozone depletion.*

Tableaux (cont.)

▸ For more complex ideas, have students create a "slideshow" in which they create multiple tableaux that show a progression. Images are presented one right after the other. The presenters can say, "Curtain down" and "Curtain up" between images, indicating that the viewers should close their eyes in between slides so that they see only the still images and not the movement between images. Viewers can share their thinking about what they have seen following each slideshow.

5. Use the *Tableaux Tips Sheet* to coach students as they're making artistic choices (side-coaching).

6. Once students have developed their ideas, have groups present their tableaux to the class. You might introduce this by saying, "Imagine we are in an art gallery. We will walk around and look at the sculptures. At each stop on our gallery walk, we will talk about what we see, brainstorm words we think of, and discuss how the tableau represents the concept."

7. Distribute the *Gallery Walk Observation Sheet* activity sheet and tell students, "We will use this to track the list of the words you use to describe what you see, and we will find out from our sculptors what the term is and how our guesses relate to the concept represented in the tableaux." Use the Discussion Questions to guide students' thinking.

8. As you move around the gallery, have students continue listing words used to describe each tableau. You may want to keep a record as well. You will end up with a rich list of adjectives, synonyms, and metaphors that will encourage students to see the scientific concepts in new ways. Add to the list as each group describes their process of creating their tableau. This is often where ideas are translated and realizations occur. Capturing students' language will reveal the connections they have made.

Discussion Questions

▸ What concept do you think is being represented, and what emotion is conveyed?

▸ What words come to mind as you view the sculpture?

▸ What do you see in the sculpture that suggests change in the environment?

▸ What cause-and-effect relationships do you see embodied in the sculpture?

▸ What similarities and differences were there in the different sculptures of the same ideas?

▸ As you were creating your tableau, how did you choose to portray environmental impact and why?

▸ What ideas from the *Tableaux Tips* were included and how?

▸ What artistic choices did you make in creating your tableau?

▸ How did the descriptions offered by the viewers of your tableau match your ideas of the concepts being presented and the emotions you wanted to evoke?

▸ In what ways did the responses expand on what was being represented?

Tableaux (cont.)

Specific Grade-Level Ideas

Grades K–2

Ask students to consider where they see human traces in their own communities (houses, garbage, cut grass, and so on). Have students imagine what the area was like before houses were there. Provide them with vocabulary or concepts that are concrete and easy to enact (such as a carefully designed garden or a fence). Have them use their bodies to create shapes that represent physical objects that contribute to different forms of pollution (air, water, ground, sound). Provide students with the opportunity to embody the idea and then develop the skills to hold a shape still.

This strategy also can be used to observe and demonstrate how plants grow and germinate as well as the factors that affect plant growth and development.

"To teach a science [concept] through drama, first introduce the science content. Then teach the arts skills and ask the students to create. Then ask students how their drama work applies to what they're learning in science class. They will tell you the connections. They will find many you had not thought of. Also, things they are confused about will come up—'Oh! The CO_2 goes in, not out. We have to change the scene.'"

—Susan Pope (n.d., para. 3)

Grades 3–5

Help students create a list of human activities that stress the physical environment, such as driving cars, disposing of waste in rivers, and generating electricity. You also can challenge students with a term such as *pollution*, which will require them to portray a general category and recognize the underlying connection among several examples. Engage students in doing research to investigate the differences between purposeful interventions and unintended consequences. Have students consider the unintended consequences of purposeful interventions such as dams or canals. Make the work interdisciplinary by inviting students to consider the social and historical consequences of such projects. This strategy can also be used to depict anything that changes over time, such as the transformation of larvae or the slow process of rock formation and deterioration. Invite students to create several tableaux in a "slideshow" that reflects the change over time.

Tableaux (cont.)

Specific Grade-Level Ideas (cont.)

Grades 6–8

Engage students in larger and more abstract ideas such as ozone depletion or climate change. Provide a list of concepts they can research independently. Ask students to consider the impact of both renewable and nonrenewable resources and challenge them to brainstorm ideas that may have a positive environmental impact or that may reverse some of the damage. Ask students to create a sense of suspense as they investigate potential environmental crises, tension as they work through difficult solutions, and hopefulness as they find ways to avert future crises. This strategy can be used to investigate and represent larger environmental changes such as geological changes in the earth and the forces that cause them. Invite students to discuss their artistic choices in creating images depicting abstract ideas.

Grades 9–12

Have students focus on a particular ecosystem and the variable factors that negatively impact that ecosystem. For example, students can explore the causes and environmental impact of harmful algal blooms (HABs), which result from the increased presence of phytoplankton and cyanobacteria in coastal waters. Students can investigate the impact on human life on the ecosystem itself (for example, disruptions in food webs or mass mortality), on surrounding wildlife, and on socioeconomic motives (tourism, commercial fisheries, or public health, for example). Students also could investigate the harmful effects of deforestation on major rain forests across the globe among other intricate ecosystems. Students can create tableaux to show cause and effect, and discuss the changes that occur moving from one to the other.

Name: _____ Date: _____

Tableaux Tips

As you create your tableau, consider using elements of focus, action, space, and levels to create a compelling and dramatic image.

Focus: As you create your image, identify where you want the viewers' eyes to go. Create/compose your tableau in a way that creates a sense of focus to help the viewers notice what is most important first.

Action: Your image is still, but you want to create a sense of an active moment captured in time. Think of your tableau as an active moment that was paused right in the middle of the action.

Space: Your tableau is a frozen sculpture. Harness the power of a three-dimensional image by using space intentionally.

Levels: Arranging people's bodies on different levels makes the tableau more interesting. See the following suggestions.

Using Levels in Drama

Levels	Frozen Movements
low level	crawling, crouching, rolling, crab walking
mid level	bending, walking hunched over, skipping, skating, sliding, swimming through air
high level	reaching, jumping, walking on tiptoes

Source: Monica Prendergast. Used with permission.

Name: _____ Date:_____

Gallery Walk Observation Sheet

Directions: As you watch each tableau, record your observations in the chart.

Observation Notes	Tableau 1	Tableau 2	Tableau 3
Words to describe the tableau			
Notes from the creators about their artistic choices			
The theme represented			
What I've learned about the theme			

Monologue

Model Lesson: Meet Greta Thunberg

Overview

In this lesson, students use monologue to deeply understand a well-known person or character within the field of science or engineering to learn about the diversity of the people, places, and teams that play roles in the discovery process. Using information from a variety of sources, students write and perform a monologue in which they take the perspective of a famous figure. Speaking directly to the audience, students reveal a conflict, a choice to be made, or a problem to be resolved.

Materials

- a collection of texts about your chosen scientific figure
- *Affecting History* (page 79)
- *Sample Monologue: Greta Thunberg* (page 80)
- *Monologue Planner* (page 81)
- *Elements of Drama* (page 59)

Standards

Grades K–2

- Knows that in science it is helpful to work with a team and share findings with others
- Contributes ideas for dialogue and plot while collaborating on character development
- Uses voice, gesture, and movement to communicate emotions

Grades 3–5

- Knows that people of all ages, backgrounds, and groups have made contributions to science and technology throughout history
- Collaborates to devise original ideas for a drama/theater work
- Makes physical choices to develop a character and create meaning

Grades 6–8

- Knows that people with diverse interests, talents, and motivations engage in science and engineering; some people work in teams and others work alone, but all communicate with others
- Develops a character by considering inner thoughts, objectives, and motivations
- Uses various physical choices and character objectives in a collaborative drama work

Grades 9–12

- Understands that science involves different types of work in many different disciplines
- Understands that most scientists and engineers work in teams to design, test, and refine their work
- Refines a dramatic concept to demonstrate understanding of historical and cultural influences of ideas applied to a drama work

Monologue (cont.)

Preparation

Gather a collection of texts by different authors that focus on scientific figures. The collection may include biographies, research articles, historical fiction, poetry, primary sources, and more. Subjects could include current scientific researchers such as Jane Goodall, Katy Payne, E. O. Wilson, Stephen Hawking, or Tyrone Hayes, or historical figures such as Diane Fossey, Rosalind Franklin, or Rachel Carson.

Use the *Sample Monologue: Greta Thunberg* and practice reading the monologue aloud, or select an example from literature to share with students. If students are not familiar with what a monologue is, share a selection from a familiar play or movie. You might find resources such as *Magnificent Monologues for Kids 2* by Chambers Stevens and *Minute Monologues for Kids* by Ruth Mae Roddy to be helpful. Additional suggestions are provided in the Specific Grade-Level Ideas.

Procedure

1. Divide the class into groups and assign each a scientific figure to explore through monologue. Distribute the *Affecting History* activity sheet to each group. Explain that they will research a historical figure using multiple sources and considering different perspectives. Provide students with access to the collection of resources you gathered and direct students to review several sources of information about the same person and record their findings on the *Affecting History* activity sheet. Circulate and facilitate group work as needed.

2. Bring the class together to share students' work. Tell students that they will present the information they learned through monologue. Talk with students about how a monologue is different from a dialogue.

3. Read the *Sample Monologue: Greta Thunberg* (or your chosen example) to students *without* dramatic flair.

4. Reread the monologue, asking students to close their eyes and visualize the character as you add dramatic flair to the reading. How might the character look, talk, move, or behave? Ask students for suggestions on how you could read the monologue dramatically. For example, when might you change your voice, make a gesture, move, pause, or otherwise dramatize the reading? Model these ideas in another reading of the monologue. Discuss what students were able to learn about the character through the monologue and the way you presented it.

5. Distribute the *Monologue Planner* activity sheet and provide time for students to begin planning their individual monologues.

6. Have students share their monologue ideas with their group and think about which ideas suggest a conflict, which ideas could lead to effective dramatization, and which ideas might suggest humor or emotion.

7. Provide time for students to develop their monologues based on their expanded ideas.

8. Have students present their monologues to the class. Debrief the monologues, using the Discussion Questions.

Monologue *(cont.)*

Discussion Questions

▸ What insights did you gain into the subject?

▸ What character traits came through?

▸ What is the subject wrestling with?

▸ What emotions did you feel as you experienced the monologue?

▸ Where do you see the character traits (e.g., boldness) come through in the monologue?

▸ In what ways does the subject stay true to their ideals?

▸ What sources were helpful? What biases did you discover?

▸ Now that you know the subject, are there other motivations that come to mind that could inform their future choices?

▸ Did the subject take risks to solve a problem? How?

Specific Grade-Level Ideas

Grades K–2

The activity can be more improvisational for younger students. When giving students a specific context, it helps them to consider how their chosen person would react in that situation. Assign students a science subject that they have prior knowledge of, such as person or animal you have studied. Ask students to imagine they are the science subject they chose, entering a party where nobody knows them. How would they introduce themselves as that subject? What is important about how they look or where they can be found? Students can begin their monologues by saying, "Hi, I'm (name of character). Let me tell you a bit about myself." Imagine that the character has something important on their mind. What might it be?

Students can create monologues about things other than people, such as plants, animals, rocks, or planets.

"Drama in science models ways in which scientists develop and validate theories and provides a productive platform for debating the social, political and cultural dimensions of science, that help give science a human face, especially for students skeptical of its worth."

—Marianne Ødegaard (2003, as cited in Braund and Reiss, 2019, para. 41)

Monologue (cont.)

Specific Grade-Level Ideas (cont.)

Grades 3–5

Students may choose to perform their monologues sharing their process for invited guests. Help them practice improvising their monologue. Have them write their monologues on index cards so memorizing the lines doesn't become more important than the exploration of character. Once students become deeply familiar with a person through rehearsing their monologue, they will be able to accurately improvise the piece. Having index cards available may help the performers relax as they share their work with an audience.

Students also could create monologues from the perspective of inanimate objects in a scientist's life, such as Jane Goodall's camera, her pencil recording the behavior of the chimpanzees, or the tree where the chimps rest at night.

Grades 6–8

Have students create monologues from the point of view of other people, things, or settings in their chosen person's life, such as Tyrone Hayes's microscope, a chimpanzee within a troop studied by Jane Goodall, or Stephen Hawking's computer. Explore people from the same period in history or the same profession and invite students to write monologues from their points of view. Compare the character traits of these people through monologue.

Grades 9–12

Have students consider the work that goes into scientific and engineering research by identifying individuals often not mentioned in research teams, such as Rosalind Franklin in the discovery of the DNA double helix, the team of researchers supporting Jane Goodall, or the team supporting Stephen Hawking. Have the students explore monologue through the eyes of a team member.

Name: _____ Date: _____

Affecting History

Directions: Complete the chart to learn about a scientific figure and to consider the sources of information.

Scientific figure: _____

Describe the source of information.	Describe the person's character traits, ideas, actions, and key decisions or conflicts the person encountered in their work.	How does this information compare to information from other sources?

Sample Monologue: Greta Thunberg

They call me the climate warrior. They're missing the point. The focus should not be on me or my activism. The focus needs to be on the crises that will destroy our future.

The fact is I see the world changing in ways that concern me. Change is coming whether we like it or not.

I learned about climate change in school. Starving polar bears, the warming of the planet, the droughts, and the unpredictable weather patterns. . . . The stories were alarming—and true—and backed by science.

It unmoored me. My teacher and classmates moved on to other topics, but I could not. I stopped eating. I stopped speaking. I couldn't imagine why people were naming the crisis but didn't care enough to act. Why aren't people talking about this? Why isn't it a priority? If I care about something, I go all in. And yet I seemed alone in this.

I saw our "leaders" focusing on stories of success, with no thought about the environmental price tag that comes with the choices they are making. I thought, "We are in the beginning of a mass extinction, and all you can talk about is money and fairy tales of eternal economic growth. . . . How dare you!?"

I said, "You say you love your children above all else. And yet you are stealing their future in front of their very eyes."

It may seem distant to you but I am . . . the young people are . . . the ones who will be affected.

We have failed when it comes to climate change.

We say it's important and it's urgent . . . but. there's. no. action.

So I went on strike . . . stopped going to school in protest. I sat all by myself in front of Parliament with a sign I made that said "School Strike for Climate." And I was alone for a long time. And then one day someone joined me. And then a few more, and then a few dozen. A movement began.

So now I speak what I believe, and the demonstrations have followed. Now I see thousands of children standing up, leaving class for "Fridays for Future," drawing attention to the crisis. It gives me hope.

Our leaders are acting like children. And so it's us—young people. We are the ones who will need to take responsibility. We can't just continue living as if there was no tomorrow, because there is a tomorrow.

Science tells the story we are ignoring. Oceans will rise. Cities will flood. Millions of people will suffer.

The world is waking up. I want to tell my grandchildren that we did everything we could.

I'm 16. I'm not a political leader. I'm not an advocacy group. I'm not the only one to be concerned about the climate crisis. I'm not the one who is qualified to fix the issues we face. I'm a teenager who is speaking about things I care about. I'm taking action on things I worry about.

And you should, too.

Visualization by Lisa Donovan. Used by permission.

References Used When Writing This Monologue:
Alter, Charlotte, Syun Haynes, and Justin Worland. 2019. "Person of the Year 2019—Greta Thunberg." *Time*, December, 2019. time.com/person-of-the-year-2019-greta-thunberg/.
PBS Newshour. 2019. "Climate Activist Greta Thunberg on the Power of a Movement." www.pbs.org/video/climate-warrior-1568414322/.

Name: _____ Date: _____

Monologue Planner

Directions: Answer the questions to help plan your monologue.

What character traits does the person show? How?	How old is the person? Where does the person live?
What type of research does the person do? In what setting (with a team, in a lab, or out in the field)? How is this important?	What challenge, decision, or dilemma does the person face?
What is the person trying to reveal?	How does the person feel about what they are saying? What facial expressions and body stances could portray this feeling?
How will your voice change to reflect emotion and character?	What will the person realize at the end of the monologue?

Mantle of the Expert

Model Lesson: Designing an Animal Sanctuary

Overview

In this strategy, students problem-solve in the role of a designer to create a sanctuary for rescued animals. Students present their ideas, and, to probe each group's vision further, they answer questions about their design asked by fellow classmates who are acting as administrators, animal behaviorists, and wildlife educators.

Materials

- books, images, videos, or other materials about animal habitats and ecosystems
- information about local, regional, and national animal sanctuaries
- *Animal Sanctuary Director Memo* (page 86)
- *Brainstorming Guide* (page 87)
- *Presentation Guide* (page 88)
- *Elements of Drama* (page 59)

Standards

Grades K–2

- Describes what resources plants and animals need to survive
- Describes habitats where some organisms survive well, some survive less well, and some cannot survive at all
- Collaborates to develop a guided drama experience communicate emotions

Grades 3–5

- Constructs a scientific explanation for how an ecosystem's food web supports the growth of plants and animals
- Makes a claim that when the environment changes, the types of plants and animals that live there may change
- Collaborates to develop and present a drama/theater work

Grades 6–8

- Constructs a scientific explanation based on evidence for how organisms interact and depend on one another in an ecosystem
- Understands how descriptions, dialogue, and actions are used to discover, articulate, and justify
- Demonstrates mutual respect for self and others while incorporating ideas to develop and present a drama/theater work

Grades 9–12

- Uses evidence to support comparison of the relationships among interdependent organisms that affect the stability and capacity of ecosystems
- Evaluates the claims, evidence, and reasoning that biological magnification in ecosystems changes conditions and may result in a new ecosystem
- Communicates directorial choices for improvised or scripted scenes

Mantle of the Expert (cont.)

Preparation

Identify animal sanctuaries in your area. Sanctuaries provide safe and secure homes for all sorts of animals in need, such as farm animals, pets, draft horses, greyhounds, sheep, pigs, cows, chickens, pigeons, exotic animals, wolves, and more. Locate books, images, videos, and other information related to each animal sanctuary in your area or beyond. Students will explore a diverse array of habitats (desert, ocean, river, jungle), animal types (dolphin, gorilla, snake, spider), or a collection of animals across one habitat. If time allows, visit animal sanctuaries in person or online to give students ideas about how to best proceed.

Read the *Animal Sanctuary Director Memo* and decide if you will use it as written or adapt it to meet the needs of students. If you decide to use the memo as written, customize it for each group by adding the animal name and presentation date to the memo.

Determine how you will group students as they create plans for sanctuary habitats. Groups of three or four are suggested. Give at least two groups the same animal or concept, which will serve to show how an engineering design can be approached from different perspectives. Sharing a similar focus also deepens the knowledge of the group in a particular area so that when students are watching other presentations, they will be able to ask in-depth questions of the panels. Additional suggestions are provided in the Specific Grade-Level Ideas.

> "Mantle of the Expert does not mean the students are magically endowed with expertise. In the real world they are still children. It is only inside the fiction they work 'as if' they are experts. That is in the sense that they take on the powers and responsibilities of a team of experts, working on important assignments, caring about the things they do, and taking pride in their status."
>
> —Mantle of the Expert (n.d., para. 1)

Procedure

1. Research and share examples of animal sanctuaries in your area.

2. Invite students to imagine that they work at an animal sanctuary and have been asked to replicate the natural habitat of one of the animals. Explain that their role will consist of brainstorming ideas to provide a habitat for the animal.

3. Tell students they will receive a memo from the director of the animal sanctuary explaining their next design assignment.

4. Divide the class into small groups. Assign an animal to each group. Distribute the *Animal Sanctuary Director Memo* to each group. Have students read the memo and discuss the animal they have been assigned.

5. Distribute the *Brainstorming Guide* activity sheet and have students complete it with their groups.

6. Check in with groups as they work and listen to their preliminary ideas. Help them shape their design concepts for the habitat and prompt them to consider how to present their design ideas. Use the Planning Questions to guide students' thinking. Provide resource materials for students to share or have them gather their own.

7. Once groups have identified their concepts, ask them to think of their role, the challenges that may arise, and how their design will address the needs of the animal(s) and education of the public. Distribute the *Presentation Guide* activity sheet and ask students to think about and record the sequence in which they want to describe their design ideas to the class. Provide time for groups to rehearse their presentations. While they practice, circulate among the groups and provide feedback.

Mantle of the Expert (cont.)

8. Tell students that as each group presents, students not involved in the presentation will act as an environmental board approving selection of what will be included in the new animal sanctuary. Invite groups to present their ideas to the panel. Direct each group to introduce the designers in their group and present their ideas in a dramatic presentation. During the presentation, the panel should write questions to ask during a question-and-answer period following the presentation.

9. Facilitate a final discussion in which designers and administrators note the features of the presentations that were most effective and compelling, focusing on the animal needs and public education.

10. Use the Discussion Questions to debrief the experience.

Planning Questions

▸ Describe what the animals need to thrive in an ecosystem.

▸ How will you design an environment that will meet the needs of the animals?

▸ What do you need to know?

▸ What examples can you use from the sanctuaries you've researched?

▸ How can you use your expertise as an animal sanctuary designer to convince administrators that this design deserves to be created?

▸ How will you engage the public with education and advocacy and request financial support?

▸ How will you use creative problem-solving to solve the problem?

▸ How will you present your research as you act as an expert in the field?

Discussion Questions

▸ How did taking on the role of an expert feel? Why?

▸ How did it feel to be a member of the panel?

▸ In what ways was taking on the role of the designer different from presenting information as a student?

▸ What ideas from other areas of science did you use to help you solve the problem?

Mantle of the Expert (cont.)

Specific Grade-Level Ideas

Grades K–2

Invite students to think of themselves as scientists who study a particular animal. Tell students that a designer of a sanctuary for their animal will be coming to interview them about the needs and habitat to inform their design. As teacher you can take on the role of the designer; in role, ask students to help you to understand the specific needs of their animal.

Additional topics include designing a museum exhibit on racecars or a park. For the park, students can target how to best capture daily temperature and sun/shade areas. See **pbskids.org/designsquad/** for more ideas.

Grades 3–5

Have students design habitat enrichment components for local animals, such as a butterfly garden, birdhouses, or bat boxes. Students must research what kind of food or nesting components are needed for that particular species within the local habitat and then determine the best area to add the enrichment components and observe the changes in behavior.

Grades 6–8

Have students select a scientific invention (recent or historical) and imagine they are an expert in the science topic, concepts, or technology behind the invention. Explain to students that they have been invited to address a local elementary school and must share the science topic/concept/technology related to the invention in language that is easy for students to understand. If desired, give classmates the opportunity to ask the "experts" questions about the invention and/or the science concepts.

Grades 9–12

Invite students to pick a complex topic such as climate change. Have them identify three experts related to the topic, such as a marine biologist, an environmental scientist, and a meteorologist. Ask students to take on a role and conduct additional research to support their expertise. Place them in a scenario (documentary, talk show, or interview) and encourage them to share their expertise on the topic in ways appropriate to that context.

Name: _____ Date: _____

Animal Sanctuary Director Memo

To: Animal Sanctuary Design Team

From: Animal Sanctuary Director

Re: Animal Enrichment Design Idea Development

Congratulations! Based on your expertise in habitat design, your team has been selected to plan and design a new animal sanctuary for rescued

_____ .

You will present your ideas on _____ (date). Please be prepared to make a compelling case for your proposed habitat and answer questions from the board.

Your design should focus on the needs of a single animal species: habitat needs, food webs, and requirements for the survival and flourishing of the species.

Please find time to meet with your team, research habitat dynamics, and develop good examples of what might be included.

Good luck, and I look forward to hearing your creative conservation ideas.

Name: _____ Date: _____

Brainstorming Guide

Directions: Fill in the chart to organize your ideas for your habitat. Attach sketches of potential layouts.

Animal species:
Habitat:
Initial ideas:

Questions to Consider	Ideas
What do animals need to thrive in this habitat?	
What specific design features address animal needs?	
How might you educate the public about the animals and their habitat as part of your plan for the sanctuary?	

Name: _____ Date: _____

Presentation Guide

Directions: Complete the chart to organize your ideas for your exhibit presentation.

Presentation title:		
Animal species:		
Animal Habitat Design		
Drawings	Props	
Ecosystem requirements		_____ minutes
Visitor Education Focus		
Drawings	Props	
Scientific concept	Habitat component	_____ minutes
		Total time. _____ minutes

Teacher in Role

Model Lesson: The Designing Engineer

Overview

In this strategy, students imagine they are engineers who are skilled in designing new modes of transportation. Taking on the role of an engineer engages students in a meaningful exchange of ideas and sorting of scientific and technological information common to engineering work. This exchange gives the teacher and students the opportunity to address common misconceptions.

Materials

- *Design Engineer Script* (page 93)
- engineer props (props for role and project bag with design examples)
- *Engineering Evidence Chart* (page 94)
- *Elements of Drama* (page 59)

Standards

Grades K–2

- Uses materials to design a device that solves a problem
- Plans and prepares improvisations
- Predicts how characters might react and behave based on character traits
- Uses voice, gesture, and movement to communicate emotions

Grades 3–5

- Describes a simple problem that can be solved through the development of a new or improved object
- Develops a simple sketch or drawing of an invention to solve a given problem
- Predicts how characters might react and behave based on character traits
- Makes physical choices to develop a character and create meaning

Grades 6–8

- Uses inquiry and compares possible solutions to a problem based on how well each is likely to meet the criteria and constraints of the problem
- Develops an improvised character by considering inner thoughts and motivations
- Uses physical choices and character objectives in a collaborative drama work

Grades 9–12

- Designs a solution to a real-world problem by breaking it down into problems that can be solved through engineering
- Evaluates a solution to a real-world problem
- Develops an improvised character by considering inner thoughts and motivations
- Uses physical choices and character objectives in a collaborative drama work

Teacher in Role (cont.)

Preparation

Review the *Design Engineer Script* activity sheet so that you are comfortable in the role. Adapt the script as needed for your students and area of focus. Feel free to use a different speech pattern if you prefer—just make sure your delivery is different from usual to create a dramatic sense of character. As you invent your engineer persona, consider the following questions: *Who are you? What do you like? What might you wear?* Remember: You are a creative individual. You can make the activity more engaging by using props and addressing how the engineer who you invented might dress. Store props outside the classroom before you launch the activity. Your willingness to be dramatic will intrigue students and help them feel comfortable taking dramatic risks.

Gather images or small replicas of current modes of transportation, such as high-speed electric trains, automobiles (gas, hybrid, and electric), airplanes (with engines and glider), and rockets. Place them in a folder or box to share with students. Additional suggestions are provided in the Specific Grade-Level Ideas.

Procedure

1. Tell students that they will enter a drama that invites them to design and engineer a new method of transportation called New Motion that relies on renewable energy sources. Tell students that the scene will begin when you say, "Curtain up," and it will end when you say, "Curtain down."

2. Excuse yourself from the room and put on your engineer outfit. Say, "Curtain up" as you enter, letting students know that the drama is beginning. Clearly transition into the engineer role as you introduce yourself. Present the challenge to students using the *Design Engineer Script* activity sheet.

3. End the drama by telling students that their teacher is returning, but you'll be back tomorrow at the same time to see what they have collected. Say, "Curtain down" and leave the room when you are done to alert students the drama is ending. You can return later in role as the engineer to discuss the scientific and engineering concepts students arrived at in their designs.

4. Provide students time to collect images and information about current modes of transportation and to design the new method of transportation, New Motion. You may extend the activity throughout the day by challenging students to find examples in other parts of the school and at home.

5. Return to class in the engineer role, and invite students to present their design ideas. Encourage students to report in the role of experts and use their designs to convince you and their peers of their ideas. During the presentations, display the *Engineering Evidence Chart* activity sheet and use it to catalogue the designs as students present their findings. Invite other student engineers to weigh in on the discussion of designs, developing the collective knowledge of the group. Continue to add words, phrases, and significant ideas to the *Engineering Evidence Chart* activity sheet.

6. Challenge students' thinking by returning to class in the role of engineer and asking follow-up questions, such as "Can you help me identify the fastest mode of transportation that you found? Can you explain how you were effective in creating so many new designs? It has been said that some motion takes no energy to produce. What can we say to stop this rumor?"

Teacher in Role (cont.)

7. Use the Discussion Questions to explore how the various roles supported students' learning.

Discussion Questions

▸ How did you act differently when you were in the design engineer role?

▸ On what did you base your ideas about what a design engineer might be like?

▸ How did being in the design engineer role help you think in new ways about the information and the work?

▸ How was your teacher in the engineer role different from your teacher in the teacher role?

"Among drama strategies to enhance science learning, role-plays of the physical kind, where students portray molecules, components of biological cells or model processes such as energy or behaviour of electrons in circuits, offer particular advantage."

—Martin Braund and Michael J. Reiss (2019, para. 42)

Specific Grade-Level Ideas

Grades K–2

Students can design fantasy vehicles, such as rocket ships, and imagine the effect these new vehicles would have on their own lives. How would the roads have to change? Could they travel to see loved ones far away in one second? How would this impact their lives? It also may be helpful to review the meaning of the word *expert* prior to this activity and give students the opportunity to identify some ways in which they are experts. As one student suggested, "In my family, I am the expert at making my baby sister laugh." At this level, the design engineer might be a puppet that visits regularly during the course of the year, looking for examples of scientific concepts being studied at that time. This strategy also can be used to investigate the expertise of other scientists, such as a botanist looking at the variations of plants in their local area.

Grades 3–5

Discuss the role of experts and engineers prior to the activity. Ask students what they know about experts and engineers and how they can be identified. Be sure to discuss the needs and desires new technology will address. As they develop their designs, students may want to look at how our needs have changed as they look at existing technologies and where they fall short. Ask students to consider how these technologies could be used in other unexpected ways.

This strategy also can be used to imagine other challenges, such as a geologist investigating new ways to extract renewable energy from the earth.

Teacher in Role *(cont.)*

Specific Grade-Level Ideas *(cont.)*

Grades 6–8

Students can collect engineering design ideas from newspapers and store flyers. Challenge students to mirror the scientific inquiry method as they work on their designs. Have them propose solutions, develop some sketches, and investigate the scientific concepts behind their design. Do the scientific data support the feasibility of their design? Are there unintended consequences with significant negative impact? Once they have developed their designs, they can present their own design engineering role-play to younger students.

The strategy could be used to teach other content areas such as cell biology, where the teacher takes on the role of a cell biologist searching for gene-based medical remedies.

Grades 9–12

Have students investigate different modes of transportation by analyzing the progression of technological improvements in terms of speed, efficiency, and sustainability. In doing this, students can track mankind's use of renewable and nonrenewable resources as it relates to modes of transportation (for example, a shipbuilder's use of wood, a sailor's use of wind power, the use of fossil fuels to power automobiles, or a steam locomotive's use of coal). Then students can offer proposed improvements to these modes of transportation in the role of experts from the time period. If desired, group students according to the criteria they will investigate (for example, speed, efficiency, sustainability, or mode of transportation), and have groups compare and contrast their findings about transportation technology over time and sustainable transportation practices.

Design Engineer Script

Curtain up.

(*Engineer peers around the corner curiously, as if looking for something.*)

Good! You have arrived. (*Insert teacher's name*) told me you would be here and be ready to work on my design. I need your help!

I am a design engineer. Who knows what a design engineer does? I have been asked to design (*looks confused as if trying to recall important information*) a new method of transportation, *New Motion*! That's right. *New Motion*, a new form of locomotion, a new mode of transportation. I am not entirely sure if I know exactly what that might be, but never fear! Design engineers design!

I really hope that you will join me as design engineers in training. You will learn that it takes great observation and focus to be a designer. You never know what you will be asked to find. People, things, scientific and technological information of all kinds. . . .

(*Looks around the room carefully.*) Perhaps you know what locomotion is. And you also might know some current forms of transportation. Well, I really need your help. You see, I have one tiny problem. I . . . well . . . that's the thing I never quite learned in school, so I really don't know what to look for! Will you help me?

I need to know what locomotion looks like and what forms of transportation are in use now. How will I recognize them? I need this information so I can—so we can—design New Motion. Can you help? Just to make sure we are on the same page, let's list the characteristics of locomotion and transportation that we need to know for *New Motion*.

(*Discussion ensues as the engineer works with students to determine where they may find examples of locomotion that transport people. As student engineers make relevant points, sharing their knowledge about concepts and examples, the design engineer takes notes on the board. These words and phrases can be referred to when they return together with examples of locomotion in hand.*)

Great! Thank you! I now know what I am looking for. I think I have a few examples in my bag that fit the description of the evidence you have described. Let's see. . . .

(*At this point, the engineer can pull out examples and share them to solidify students' understanding of what they are looking for.*)

Your job is to locate and document examples of transportation and locomotion, and then you must design new modes of transportation, or *New Motion*. You will work in groups. We will meet later to share what we have found.

But *shhhh*! Your teacher is coming back—can we keep my mission a secret? Will you help me find examples of locomotion so we can design *New Motion*? See you tomorrow. Oh, and good luck!

Curtain down.

Name: _____ Date: _____

Engineering Evidence Chart

Directions: Complete the chart.

Engineering content:	
Description of Design Evidence	**Description of Engineering Concepts**

Poetry

Poetry

Understanding Poetry

Poetry engages students in writing, reading, speaking, and listening. Creating poems can capture the essence of an idea. As stated by Polly Collins, "When students create poems about topics of study, they enhance their comprehension through the connections they have made between the topic and their own lives, the topic and the world around them, and the poetry and the content texts they have read" (2008, 83). Developing scientific understanding through the creation of poems challenges students to consider concepts related to science in new ways and to share their understanding through language and metaphor. Often students enjoy creating poems but are not sure how to begin. The strategies provide guidance that will help students identify and work with rich language to explore scientific ideas. Though poems often rhyme, they do not need to, and sentences do not always need to be complete. "We are more interested in 'surprising images' or words that have a special sound pattern. They empower students to be 'word-gatherers'" (McKim and Steinbergh 1992). Students are invited to put words together in unconventional ways, drawing on evocative language and the playful juxtaposition of ideas, and create images through words as they write poems about concepts in science. This active engagement changes students' relationships with science as they find their own language to describe what they know and observe.

We tend to think about science as working with facts and formulas, and yet theoretical structures of science, its vocabulary, and the application to real-world situations are equally important for students to understand. By working with poetic language, symbolism and metaphor, students can deepen and articulate their understanding of scientific ideas.

Using poetry to explore scientific ideas builds conceptual understanding. When students become poets, they fine-tune their writing and explore the use of patterns, rhythm that is also found in scientific concepts, and metaphor, which has the capacity to make scientific principles visible. Writing poems allows students to use language in fresh ways to develop a deeper understanding of scientific ideas. As Arthur D. Efland (quoted in Stewart and Walker 2005) notes, "It is only in the arts where the processes and products of the imagination are encountered and explored in consciousness—where they become objects of inquiry, unlike in the sciences where the metaphors that are used remain hidden" (111).

Elements of Poetry

The following list of terms related to poetry is informed by the Academy of American Poets (n.d.), and the work of Kwame Alexander (2019), Georgia Heard (1999), and Mary Oliver (1994).

- **Sound:** The creation of meaning with sound, often through the use of onomatopoeia, assonance, consonance, alliteration, and more.

- **Rhythm:** The beat of the poem, created through pattern, repetition, rhyme, syllables, and more.

- **Imagery:** Precise word choices and figurative language create an image in the reader's mind by evoking the senses and imagination.

- **Structure:** The organization of ideas. Some poems are free verse, others follow a specific form. Intentional line breaks and use of space on the page create meaning.

- **Density:** What is said (or can be said) in the space; density distinguishes poetry from regular speech and prose.

- **Audience:** Poets write with their audience in mind, revealing tone or attitude toward the message, subject, and more.

Poetry *(cont.)*

Strategies for Poetry

Poems for Two Voices

Compare and contrast is one of the most effective instructional strategies that teachers can use (Marzano 2007). A poem for two voices encourages students to explore two different perspectives on a topic. This form of poetry works well with opposite but related concepts or perspectives. Similarities and differences between concepts can be explored, providing the rhythm and feel of a dialogue. The poem is constructed by two writers, encouraging conversation about the content being explored and the ways to best translate ideas into poetic form. This collaborative work enables students to share what they know with their peers and to deepen learning. These poems also prompt students to better differentiate between two concepts being learned at the same time.

"I Am From" Poems

This biographical strategy gives students the opportunity to investigate traditions, attitudes, environmental influences, and commonly held perceptions about a particular idea or within a particular era. Inspired by George Ella Lyon (2010), "I Am From" poems follow a pattern using the phrase *I am from* and can be created through student responses to prompts (Kuta 2003). Using the senses to reflect on what has been seen, heard, smelled, touched, and tasted, students become aware of how they (or characters, fictional or real) have been shaped by their unique experiences. The observations and reflections help students become aware of how time and place can influence one's perspectives. When written about characters, students consider how context and background influence the development of a character's frame of reference.

Found Poetry

This strategy prompts students to find and collect words or phrases from a variety of sources and encourages experimentation with the placement and juxtaposition of ideas to reveal fresh language, insights, relationships, and content connections. "Found poetry refashions a nonpoetic text (newspaper article, instruction manual, dictionary entry, etc.) into poetry through lineation, excision, and collage practices" (Poetry Foundation 2015, para. 1).

McKim and Steinbergh write about the juxtaposition of words, noting, "The very fact of manipulating the words, discarding some, trading others, adding what one needs for sense, can teach us something about selection and choice in making poems. Joining two or three words that normally do not appear together can make fresh images, charging them with new energy and excitement" (1992). "Writing found poems is a structured way to have students review material and synthesize their learning" as students select language that resonates with them while organizing it around a particular topic (Facing History and Ourselves, n.d., para. 1).

Poetry (cont.)

Rhyme and Rhythm

This strategy invites students to work in verse as they translate ideas into rhyming words and phrases. Jan LaBonty notes that "a preference for rhyme and rhythm is contained in the linguistic make-up of all humans; rhyme is easier to recall than prose; rhythm helps carry the predictability of language. There is pattern and measure in every language and in the way we structure our lives" (1997). Though poems do not need to rhyme, rhymes can unify a poem, and the repeated sound can help connect a concept in one line to that in another. Also, simple rhymes can serve as a memory device (Jensen 2008) for scientific concepts, and students are even more likely to remember poems they create themselves.

Structured Poems

There are many forms of poetry that are created within specified formats. The structure of a certain number of words and syllables or a given pattern of rhythm helps students plan and organize their writing about scientific concepts. JoAnne Growney (2009) notes, "Long traditions embrace the fourteen-line sonnet with its ten-syllable lines. Five-line limericks and seventeen-syllable haiku also are familiar forms. Moreover, patterns of accent and rhyme overlay the line and syllable counts for even more intricacy" (12). The possibilities are endless as students engage with different patterns and writing within a particular structure, enabling scientific concepts to be viewed through a new lens. Furthermore, Corie Herman (2003) suggests that the structured nature of these poems supports diverse students' ability to succeed in writing them.

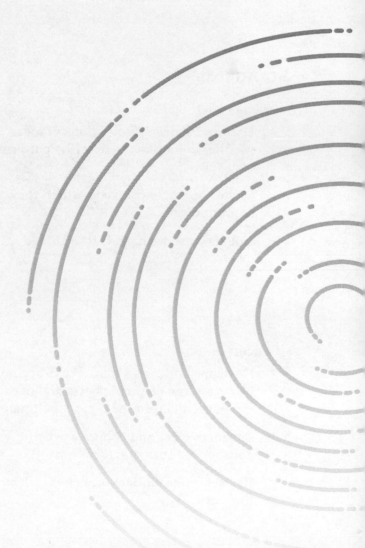

"Works of art are silent; poetry speaks its mind. Painting is mute poetry, poetry a speaking picture."

—John Hollander (2014)

Poem for Two Voices

Model Lesson: Science in Two Voices

Overview

Students read a poem written for two voices and work in pairs to create their own dialogue poems about weather and climate. As they do so, they gain a deeper understanding of the similarities and differences between the two scientific concepts. Poems for two voices also prompt students to better differentiate between two concepts that are usually learned at the same time, and thus sometimes confused, such as weather and climate.

Materials

- *Poem for Two Voices Example* (page 104)
- *Poetry Craft Tips* (page 105)
- *Poem for Two Voices Plan* (page 106)
- *Tips for Performing Poetry* (page 107)
- *Elements of Poetry* (page 97)
- voice recording technology (*optional*)

Standards

Grades K–2

- Uses and shares observations of local weather conditions to describe patterns over time
- Writes poetic narrative in which they recount events
- Collaborates with peers in a guided drama experience

Grades 3–5

- Represents data in tables and graphical displays to describe typical weather conditions expected during a particular season
- Produces clear and coherent writing appropriate to poetic form
- Collaborates with peers to revise and improve a dramatic work

Grades 6–8

- Develops and uses a model to describe how patterns of atmospheric and oceanic circulation determine regional climates
- Produces clear and coherent writing appropriate to poetic form
- Revises and refines choices in a dramatic work

Grades 9–12

- Uses a model to describe how variations in the flow of energy into and out of Earth's systems result in changes in climate
- Produces clear and coherent writing appropriate to poetic form
- Practices and revises a dramatic work

Poem for Two Voices *(cont.)*

Preparation

Familiarize yourself with the *Poem for Two Voices Example*. Note that either side of the poem is to be read by a different voice and the italicized lines are to be read by both voices.

Think about scientific ideas that are related to weather and climate but have different characteristics, such as rain and snow or conduction and convection. Focus on concepts that are most relevant to your grade level.

Brainstorm characteristics of these concepts in preparation for a discussion with students. Use the terms and phrases drawn from this process to create your own poem for two voices. This will give you the chance to foresee what students may encounter and will help you maximize your own understanding of poems for two voices so you can best guide students with appropriate resources and with the process itself. Try reading your poem aloud with an audience to get a sense of how different voices affect the meaning of the poem. Additional suggestions are provided in the *Specific Grade-Level Ideas*.

Procedure

1. Display *Poem for Two Voices Example*, or share your own poem. Have two students read the different parts of the poem aloud.

2. Ask students, "What do you notice about how this poem is written? How does the poem reveal contrasting ideas? Shared ideas? What do you notice about the quality of the spoken lines when they are read by both voices?"

3. As a class, brainstorm a list of what students know about weather and climate, and record the list for students to refer to throughout the lesson. Encourage students to use primary and secondary sources to draw out more ideas and language that might be woven into the poems.

4. Divide the class into pairs. Encourage each pair to choose two concepts for their poem from the brainstormed list. The two concepts should be different but related, such as condensation and precipitation.

5. Distribute the *Poem for Two Voices Plan* activity sheet to each pair and provide time for them to write their own poems. Circulate among students and use the Planning Questions to guide discussion. Encourage students to create an image or provide visual examples to further exemplify the concepts.

6. Provide students time to practice performing their poems aloud in two voices. As students develop their poems, encourage them to consider the content and order of the concepts they have included, and to revise based on both content and on how the poem sounds when read aloud by two voices. As needed, help students prepare to present their poems using the information in the *Tips for Performing Poetry* guide.

7. Have pairs present their poems to the rest of the class. Use the Discussion Questions to guide discussion. If desired, students can record their performances, listen to them, and discuss afterward. You also can share these poems on a class blog or by creating audio recordings.

Poem for Two Voices (cont.)

Planning Questions

▶ What words or phrases are associated with each idea?

▶ How do the perspectives differ?

▶ What ideas do the perspectives share?

▶ What could you write that the voices could read together?

▶ What powerful word choices will you use?

▶ How will you embed examples of the science within the poem?

▶ How can you illustrate the poem so that the differences between these concepts are exemplified?

Discussion Questions

▶ How did writing the poem in two voices help you identify the similarities and differences between the scientific concepts?

▶ How did listening to two separate voices help you discern the scientific concept?

▶ What did you learn about writing and articulating ideas by creating your poems?

▶ What feedback could you give the teams of authors about their poems?

Poem for Two Voices (cont.)

Specific Grade-Level Ideas

Grades K–2

Students can draw from a brainstormed list of ideas about different but related observable scientific concepts such as rain and snow or liquid and solid. As a class, brainstorm a list of descriptive words. Students are likely to focus on examples based on what they see, hear, smell, and touch. Working together to articulate what they perceive with their senses can help clarify scientific concepts. Possible topics for this strategy can include rocks and soils, the sun and moon, or plants and animals.

Grades 3–5

Have students create poems for two voices exploring related concepts such as night and day, rotation and revolution, survival and reproduction, or photosynthesis and respiration.

Grades 6–8

Students can focus on the connections and distinctions between weather and climate. Students can do some guided research to investigate the differences and connections and pull language from scientific texts. Students can create poems to compare biomes. Students can examine topics such as air and atmosphere, glaciers and icebergs, or eras and eons.

Grades 9–12

Students can conduct research and investigate the differences between internal and external energy sources that affect weather and climate. This strategy also can be used to explore any content that is related but needs to be differentiated, such as meiosis and mitosis.

Poem for Two Voices Example

Solar Eclipse	Versus	Lunar Eclipse

by Perla Diaz, with Gene Diaz

We hold both light and dark.

We are both different,	We are both the same,
sometimes light,	sometimes dark,
then changing to dark.	then changing to light.
A conundrum so stark!	A conundrum so stark!

We are seen in the sky.

When day becomes night	Shadow of third planet
in the broad daylight	revolving round the sun
sky turns from bright blue	casts darkness over light,
to the darkest hue.	moonglow undone.

Places make our appearances different.

A narrow penumbra	When light slips by
means all cannot see	we watch the night sky
the brilliant ring of fire	but only some can view
when daylight ceases to be.	full starlight of brilliant hue.

We inspire awe.

The vast ball of fire	Amidst starlit heavens
encircles black gyre.	a dark abyss appears.
People shake with fear	People tremble with wonder
when unknown is near.	the faith often asunder.

Name: _____   Date: _____

Poetry Craft Tips

Directions: Read these tips, and choose one or more to try in your poem.

- Help readers make a mental image in their mind by choosing **precise words**.
  Example: *periwinkle* instead of *blue*

- Use words that show one or more of the **five senses.**

- The decision of where to use **line breaks** impacts meaning.
  Example: Set a word or phrase on a line all by itself for impact.

- Use **alliteration** with purpose.
  Example: To show the mood or to create pacing (how quickly or slowly the reader reads a section of your poem)

- Try a **circular ending**. Begin and end your poem by repeating a word, phrase, or idea.

- **Vary the length of your stanzas**. Follow a long stanza with a short stanza (or the reverse) to show a change in events, a change within a character, the passing of time, and more.

- Repeat words or phrases to create rhythm and beat.

- Repeat words or phrases to show that an idea is important.

- Convey feelings, motivations, and action with **strong verbs.**
  Example: *dip into the water* is different from *cannonball into the water*

- Use a **metaphor** or **simile** to compare, enhancing meaning and imagination.

Source: Adapted from "Writing Strategies Used in Poetry" (pages 48-49) of *Writing Is Magic, or Is It? Using Mentor Texts to Develop the Writer's Craft* by Jennifer M. Bogard and Mary C. McMackin (2015).

Name: _____   Date:_____

Poem for Two Voices Plan

Directions: Brainstorm ideas for your poem before you begin writing. Use this planner to organize your ideas.

Summary of Event: _____

Poem Title: _____

Voice 1: _____

Voice 2: _____

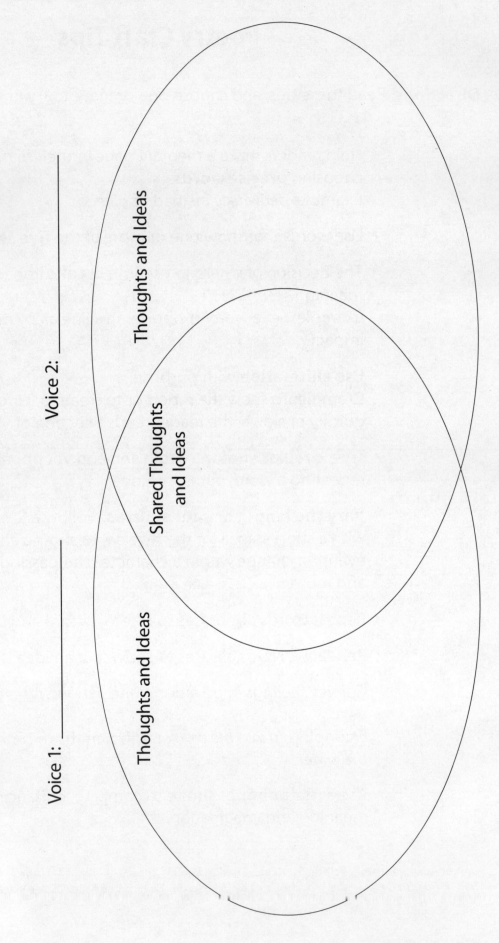

Thoughts and Ideas

Shared Thoughts and Ideas

Thoughts and Ideas

117846—Integrating the Arts in Science

Name: _____ Date: _____

Tips for Performing Poetry

Directions: Consider these helpful tips as you play around with different ways to recite a poem.

Tips to Consider

- Think about how you want your audience to feel as you recite your poem.

- Find parts that might be spoken loudly, quietly, quickly, or slowly.

- Find a place in which you can pause for added effect.

- Use facial expressions to match meaning.

- Match the tone of your voice to the meaning of the lines.

- Find places for big or small movements.

"I Am From" Poems

Model Lesson: Where I'm from Scientifically

Overview

This particular approach to a bio poem is called an "I Am From" poem. "I Am From" poems were developed by teacher and writer George Ella Lyon (2010) and suggest a simple writing prompt for exploring personal histories. An adapted format is used here for exploring scientific "I Am From" poems. Students begin each line with the phrase *I am from* and then introduce specific details of their scientific histories. The reflective process provides both students and teachers with the opportunity to find connections among students' past experiences, to note how they solve science problems and learn best, and to recognize biases they may bring to the learning of science.

Materials

- *"Where I'm from Scientifically" Examples* (page 112)
- *"Where I'm from Scientifically" Planner* (page 113)
- *Elements of Poetry* (page 97)
- *Poetry Craft Tips* (page 105)

Standards

Grades K–2

- Knows that in science it is helpful to work with a team and share findings with others
- Links events in a poetic narrative
- Demonstrates understanding of word relationships and rhyme in writing

Grades 3–5

- Knows scientists and engineers are guided by habits of mind such as intellectual honesty, tolerance of ambiguity, skepticism, and openness to new ideas
- Organizes clear and coherent writing appropriate to poetic form
- Demonstrates understanding of word relationships and rhyme in writing

Grades 6–8

- Knows scientists and engineers are guided by habits of mind such as intellectual honesty, tolerance of ambiguity, skepticism, and openness to new ideas
- Organizes clear and coherent writing appropriate to poetic form
- Demonstrates understanding of language, word relationships, and rhyme in writing

Grades 9–12

- Uses a model to describe how variations in the flow of energy into and out of Earth's systems result in changes in climate
- Produces clear and coherent writing appropriate to the task, purpose, and audience
- Demonstrates understanding of figurative language, word relationships, and nuances in word meanings

"I Am From" Poems (cont.)

Preparation

Read the *"Where I'm from Scientifically" Examples* to become familiar with how the format can be used to write a scientific autobiography or science bio poem. You also may wish to write a "Where I'm from Scientifically" poem yourself to share with students. Additional suggestions are provided in the Specific Grade-Level Ideas.

Procedure

1. Introduce the notion of being "from" someplace. Have students tell how they would respond to someone who asks casually, "Where are you from?" Then have them discuss what would be different if a good friend asked, "So how did you get to be you? What things in your life shaped or influenced you?"

2. Using the prompt "What and where is science?" have students consider their scientific learning as you brainstorm a class list about science. Encourage students to extend their thinking to the many forms that science can take and the many dimensions of scientific concepts that play out in their lives. Have students consider science concepts, history, ideas, and processes. This will give you a sense of what students understand about science, even as you expand on their ideas of what and where science may be.

3. Explain to students that they are going to write their own scientific biographies as they relate to science. Ask them about the many ways they learn about science, including school, home, movies, books, people in their lives, and so on.

4. Read aloud a bio poem from the *"Where I'm from Scientifically" Examples* and have students discuss the ways in which the author describes their scientific experiences.

5. Distribute the *"Where I'm from Scientifically" Planner* and have students discuss the various categories and possible responses. For example, they may think about their parents' attitudes toward science, their interests in science, or their expectations for learning science. You also may review the poem you read earlier in relation to the *"Where I'm from Scientifically" Planner*.

6. Allow time for students to reflect and record words, phrases, or sentences about their scientific memories.

7. Have students use their brainstormed words and phrases to create their own "Where I'm from Scientifically" poems. Be sure that students understand they don't have to include all the topics or all the words they brainstormed. Circulate among students and use the Planning Questions to guide their work.

8. Provide time for students to edit and confer about their poems in pairs and revise using *Tips for Performing Poetry*. Also have students practice presenting their poems orally to one another.

9. Have students share their poems with the class. Use the Discussion Questions to lead a discussion about the poems.

"I Am From" Poems (cont.)

Planning Questions

- ▸ What are some details about this scientific moment in your life?

- ▸ What are some other words that would help others understand how you felt about science while growing up?

- ▸ Was there a teacher who influenced you scientifically? If so, how?

- ▸ Are there stories in your life that relate to science?

- ▸ Can you include descriptions of scientific moments in your life that make your listeners feel as if they are there?

- ▸ Which poetic devices can you use (repetition, metaphor, alliteration)?

Discussion Questions

- ▸ How does this kind of poem help you learn about yourself?

- ▸ How might this kind of poem help you articulate your experience to others?

- ▸ What did you learn about the relationship of science to your life?

- ▸ What are some ways our poems are different? The same?

- ▸ What are some examples of words or phrases that helped listeners understand another person's experiences?

- ▸ What do our poems suggest about how we learn to think about science?

"I Am From" Poems (cont.)

Specific Grade-Level Ideas

Grades K–2

Students are likely learning about physical objects and exploration. Encourage them to also recognize that observation and experimentation are relevant to scientific learning. If possible, observe and record students' thinking as they develop their poems. Encourage younger students to draw pictures of scientific events rather than write about them, inviting them to develop spoken poems.

Poetry themes might include language related to materials and tools. Students also can address solutions, using known materials and tools for new designs and solutions such as microscopes.

Grades 3–5

Students can interview one another to complete the *"Where I'm from Scientifically" Planner* activity sheet. They can imagine they are reporters trying to get the real story of their classmates' scientific lives and brainstorm additional questions to draw out scientific biographies. Students can interview family and friends outside of school and recall movies or TV shows they have watched and books they have read that include scientists or scientific ideas in one way or another.

Have students work in groups to explore the living and nonliving parts that make up an ecosystem. Invite groups to write an "I Am From" poem from the perspective of their part of a given ecosystem. Invite groups to perform their poems. Follow up with a discussion of interrelationships within the ecosystem.

Grades 6–8

Students will likely have several classroom memories they can draw from. Invite them to brainstorm and describe specific incidents, but ask that they do not mention teachers' names. Encourage students to probe the thinking of several members of their family and to become sensitive to the ways in which science is portrayed in the media or by teachers of other subjects.

Students can take on the persona of a scientific concept and write an "I Am From" poem from that perspective, such as "I am an organelle. . . ." Students also could write an "I Am From" poem that examines the solar system ("I am from the solar system . . .") from the perspective of Earth, exploring its relationship to the sun and moon, the cyclical patterns of lunar phases, eclipses of the sun and moon, and seasons.

Grades 9–12

Students can explore evolution and natural selection by writing from different perspectives, such as "I am from biodiversity . . . ," exploring the similarities and differences among organisms and examining the relationship between the environment and natural selection and evolution. Poems could detail the factors causing natural selection and the process of evolution of species.

"Where I'm from Scientifically" Examples

I am from the buggy place

Ants crawl along the cracks in the sidewalk

I watch them build their homes and carry their food

I like to see the moon at night

I am from the earth

I am a scientist

—by Gene Diaz

Darwin
by Elliot Winston

I am from science

Looking farther into nature

Studying the life I see

Flourishing everywhere

The similarities between different animals

And differences between the same

I notice things overlooked by religion and

Study them in secret

The things we have discovered will change so much.

Name: _____ Date: _____

"Where I'm From Scientifically" Planner

Directions: Complete the chart by brainstorming ideas for a "Where I'm from Scientifically" poem. Then, on a separate sheet of paper, write your poem, beginning some lines with *I am from* . . .

My family and science:	What I do in my free time and science:
Words or quotes I have heard about science:	My friends and science:
How I solve science problems:	How I learn science best:

Found Poetry

Model Lesson: Scientific Word Bowls

Overview

In this lesson, students brainstorm or read about words they associate with the engineering design process and then put the terms together in new ways to create poems that depict scientific understanding. Students are encouraged to experiment with a variety of ways of juxtaposing selected words and adding others as needed.

Materials

▸ *Poetry Word List* (page 118)

▸ *Poetry Craft Tips* (page 105)

▸ *Tips for Performing Poetry* (page 107) (*optional*)

▸ *Elements of Poetry* (page 97)

▸ reusable containers or shoeboxes

▸ scissors

▸ microphone (*optional*)

Standards

Grades K–2

▸ Knows asking questions, making observations, and gathering information are parts of the design process

▸ Links events in a poetic narrative

▸ Demonstrates understanding of word relationships and rhyme in writing

Grades 3–5

▸ Knows collaboration is useful as the combination of multiple creative minds can yield more possible design solutions

▸ Organizes clear and coherent writing appropriate to poetic form

▸ Demonstrates understanding of word relationships and rhyme in writing

Grades 6–8

▸ Knows the design process relies on different strategies: creative brainstorming, evaluating the feasibility of solutions, and troubleshooting the selected design

▸ Organizes clear and coherent writing appropriate to poetic form

▸ Demonstrates understanding of language, word relationships, and rhyme in writing

Grades 9–12

▸ Knows the design process relies on different strategies: creative brainstorming, evaluating the feasibility of solutions, and troubleshooting the selected design

▸ Organizes clear and coherent writing appropriate to poetic form

▸ Demonstrates understanding of figurative language, word relationships, and nuances in word meanings

Found Poetry (cont.)

Preparation

Create a list of engineering design concepts that students are familiar with but could deepen their understanding about, such as observation, measurement, construction, testing, design, problem-solving, research, modeling, improvement, materials, systems, solutions, teamwork, and sustainability.

Decide how to group students in teams of two or three. Prepare a chart with one of the scientific design concepts listed above.

Collect reusable containers or shoeboxes to serve as word bowls. Additional suggestions are provided in the Specific Grade-Level Ideas.

Procedure

1. Have students brainstorm words that they associate with the chosen design concept. Record brainstormed words and phrases so students can refer to them throughout the lesson.

2. Ask students to help you create a class poem by selecting words and phrases from the list and arranging them into a poem. The idea is to put the words together and play with the line breaks in a variety of ways until students establish a clear sense of the ideas they are exploring. Encourage metaphors, similes, and the use of imagery, sensory descriptors, and feeling words.

3. Divide the class into small groups and assign each group an engineering design concept. Distribute the *Poetry Word List* activity sheet to each group, and have students collect words and short phrases from research materials and textbooks for powerful words and phrases to add to their lists.

4. Distribute a box, a bowl, or another container to each group to serve as a word bowl. Have students cut their words apart and place them in the word bowl.

5. Ask students to take a few words from the bowl and then work together to juxtapose the words in different ways. Remind them to pay careful attention to how the arrangement impacts meaning. Tell groups that the selected words and phrases are just a starting point to spark ideas. They can choose to not use certain words, they can draw additional words from the bowl, or they can add words and phrases they prefer.

> "Word Bowl Poems free up your imagination and give you permission to play. The more words you collect, the more of a reservoir you have for those dry days when the words just don't seem to flow on their own."
>
> —Michelle Schaub (as cited in Hershenhorn 2020, para. 7)

6. Once their poems are complete, each group should write out a final version to share with the class. Students also can add images and numbers to illustrate the ideas.

7. Allow time for students to rehearse their poems aloud to bring them to life. If desired, have students use *Tips for Performing Poetry* as a resource to help them prepare.

8. If desired, plan a poetry slam where students present their poems to a larger audience. Have students read their poems to the class. If available, bring in a microphone and invite other classes to hear the poems.

9. Use the Discussion Questions to debrief as a class.

Found Poetry *(cont.)*

Discussion Questions

▸ Why is it important to describe engineering design ideas in words?

▸ What did you learn through the process of creating a poem?

▸ What unique or fresh language came out of the exploration of juxtaposing different words and phrases?

▸ What did you learn from listening to the poems of others?

▸ How did you use artistic, expressive language to discuss and better understand science concepts?

"I tell students not to worry about rhyme or logic, but just let the words take control and lead them to new places on the page."

—Michelle Schaub (as cited in Hershenhorn 2020, para. 4)

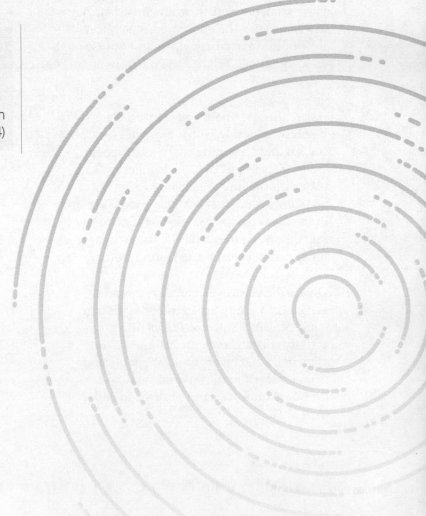

Found Poetry (cont.)

Specific Grade-Level Ideas

Grades K–2

Gather different recordings of sounds in nature, drawing from resources such as TeacherTube or National Geographic for Kids. Invite students to listen closely, brainstorming words and phrases. You also might take students outside to observe sounds around your school.

Grades 3–5

When conducting an experiment, invite students to brainstorm words and phrases based on what they see, sense, smell, hear, and feel. Collect the words as a class to create a bank of words. Play with the arrangement of the words and phrases to create a found poem.

Grades 6–8

Have students use found poetry to investigate scientific topics such as heat. Possible brainstormed words could include general terms describing heat (*hot, mixing, burning, rubbing, energy*), heat produced by burning (*fire, wood, coal, sun, light, ash*), or heat produced by rubbing things together (*friction, movement, hands, warm*). Students also may use particular ideas about heat that are relevant to them, such as a fireplace, campfire, or candle. This strategy can be used to explore other scientific topics such as weather, living organisms, or energy.

Grades 9–12

In addition to the suggestions for grades 6–8, students can use found poetry to investigate ways that heat is produced when living organisms convert stored energy to motion (*breathe, run, swim, sprout, grow, bloom*), heat that is produced when machines convert stored energy (*kinetic, engine, motor, turbine, noise, spark, gears*), conduction (*transfer, flow, gradient, thermal, diffusion*), or properties associated with heat conductivity (*insulation, thermal, conductivity, coefficient, resistivity*). This strategy also can be used to explore other topics such as the water cycle, the composition of Earth, or plant structure and growth.

Name: _____ Date: _____

Poetry Word List

Directions: Record words and short phrases about your topic in the spaces below. Then cut out the words and place them in the word bowl. Draw out a few words and arrange them in different ways. Play with the arrangement of these words and phrases to create meaning, mood, and rhythm.

My collection of words and phrases:

Rhyme and Rhythm

Model Lesson: Concept Rhymes

Overview

In this lesson, students explore the rhyme and meter of different poems about science by reading them aloud with expression. They discuss how performing poetry relies on working with the rhythm and meter of a poem. Students investigate syllables and patterns by reading aloud and playing with volume, pace, rhythm, intonation, and proper pronunciation as they bring ideas in the poem to life. Students also share their thoughts about rhyming and nonrhyming poems. Finally, students perform their favorite poems again and again, giving them the opportunity to internalize concepts in the poems.

Materials

- poetry books with rhyming and nonrhyming poems
- audio-recording software (*optional*)
- *Science Concept Poem Examples* (page 123)
- *Rhymes and Rhythms Planning Guide* (page 124)
- *My Science Concept Poem* (page 125)
- *Elements of Poetry* (page 97)
- *Poetry Craft Tips* (page 105)

Standards

Grades K–2

- Develops models to describe that organisms go through a process of growth and change
- Demonstrates understanding of word relationships and rhyme in writing

Grades 3–5

- Uses evidence to construct an explanation that living organisms have distinct structures and body systems that serve specific advantages in surviving, finding mates, and reproducing
- Demonstrates understanding of word relationships and rhyme in writing

Grades 6–8

- Develops a model that predicts and describes that waves have energy and interact with matter and can transfer energy
- Demonstrates understanding of language, word relationships, and rhyme in writing

Grades 9–12

- Explains reasoning behind the idea that electromagnetic radiation can be described either by a wave model or a particle model
- Demonstrates understanding of figurative language, word relationships, and nuances in word meanings

Rhyme and Rhythm *(cont.)*

Preparation

Gather both rhyming and nonrhyming poems. Have different poetry books available so students can choose poems of interest. If desired, have audio-recording software available for students to record and rerecord their recitations. Think about how scientific information is conceptualized and how possible misconceptions may be related. Reflect on scientific data to aid in identifying the concepts that you want students to focus on, or, if appropriate, have students identify the concepts they want to understand in more depth. Begin by thinking about how systems are often described by scientists in relation to their functions in an organism (circulatory, respiratory, and so on), and think of the other ways systems are often described (by location, by the key components, and so on). Identify examples of humorous poems that rhyme and students will enjoy. Locate at least two poems with different rhyme schemes. Review the sample poems in the *Science Concept Poem Examples*. Share these with students as models or create examples of your own. Additional suggestions are found in the Specific Grade-Level Ideas.

Procedure

1. Read aloud a poem from the *Science Concept Poem Examples* or read your selected example. As you read the poem, ask students to pay particular attention to the rhyming words and rhythmic patterns they hear. Discuss the poem with students.

2. Display the poem for students to see and ask them to identify where the rhyming words occur in the stanzas. Have students identify the rhyme scheme. Repeat this process with a second poem so students recognize that a variety of rhyming patterns are possible.

3. Divide the class into pairs and distribute the *Rhymes and Rhythms Planning Guide* to each student. Have students work together to conduct research about a science concept. Encourage students to explore multiple related science concepts to deepen their understanding of a single concept before writing. Then have students brainstorm rhyming words and rhythmic patterns that relate to the science concept, such as human body systems. Students should work together to gather ideas, but each student should record the ideas on their own sheet of paper.

4. Tell students that they will independently write a poem using the rhyming words and/or rhythms they recorded. Distribute the *My Science Concept Poem* activity sheet. Provide time for students to create, edit, and illustrate their poems. Circulate among students as they work and use the Planning Questions to stimulate students' thinking.

5. Provide time for students to practice reading their poems aloud with rhythm and intonation. Then have students read their poems aloud to the class. Post students' poems in the classroom for them to refer to later, thus increasing the likelihood of understanding and recall.

6. Use the Discussion Questions to debrief the activity.

Rhyme and Rhythm *(cont.)*

Planning Questions

▸ What scientific ideas will you include in your poem?

▸ How might you incorporate rhyme?

▸ How might you incorporate rhythm?

▸ How will you work to match the rhythm of the syllables in each line?

▸ What image(s) will you use to illustrate your concept poem?

Discussion Questions

▸ What elements created the patterns (syllables, alliteration, onomatopoeia)?

▸ What sensory details brought the poem to life?

▸ What metaphors and/or similes were effective?

> "There's something about reciting rhythmical words aloud—it's almost biological—that comforts and enlivens human beings."
>
> —Robert Pinsky (as cited in Keillor 2006, para. 4)

Rhyme and Rhythm (cont.)

Specific Grade-Level Ideas

Grades K–2

"The Drinking Fountain" by Marchette Chute or "The Secret Place" by Tomie dePaola are good poems to introduce this activity. Students can write poems about simple concepts, such as grouping organisms (plants, animals, nonliving objects) or the life cycles of different organisms. Their rhymes are likely to be exact rhymes of one-syllable words, such as *plant* or *leaf.*

Grades 3–5

"Messy Room" by Shel Silverstein and "Children's Party" by Ogden Nash are good poems to introduce this activity. The book *The Beauty of the Beast: Poems from the Animal Kingdom* by Jack Prelutsky contains poems organized by biological classification categories. Students can write poems about concepts that require memorization, such as the phases of the water cycle.

Grades 6–8

In addition to poems listed earlier, students at this level also enjoy "The Cloud" by Percy Shelley. Have students create poems that show a sophisticated understanding of human body systems or other concepts, such as Earth systems (layers of the atmosphere, factors that impact the climate, tilt of Earth's axis and seasons) or properties of matter (molecular arrangement and motion, chemical reactions).

Grades 9–12

Have students write poems about the periodic table of the elements. For example, students could write rhyming and/or rhythmic poems that explore the characteristics of noble gases or halogens, noting the similarities and differences the elements share in the structure of the poem. Students also could use this strategy to delve into the different ionic and covalent bonds, using rhyme and rhythm as a vehicle for comparing the similarities, the differences, the respective strengths and weaknesses of either bond, and the respective stability of either bond.

Science Concept Poem Examples

Grades K–2

The Butterfly

He eats and eats and eats
and eats
And spins into a chrysalis
From caterpillar to winged
delight
An amazing metamorphosis

Grades 3–5

Who Knew?

In science today,
I realized I
rely upon alveoli
inside my lungs
where millions live,
an amazing contribution
to life they give,
these little hollow cavities
at the terminal end
of the respiratory tree
where pumping blood
by sacs will pass
and on the way
exchange gas.
CO_2 leaves through diffusion,
absorbing oxygen,
reducing confusion!
Ah, the structure of anatomy.

Grades 6–8

Flashbulb

Flash!
Reflect, refract, absorb
Photo has an orb
blur of light
circle of white
light
bounces off solid particles
on my camera lens
light bends
can be a
cause for celebration
when there's a chromatic
aberration

Grades 9–12

Earthquake

Tectonic plates shift
Seismographs record data:
Earthquake predicted.

Light and Sound

Light
Color, intensity
Reflecting, refracting, absorbing
Electromagnetic, visible, audible,
    kinetic
Absorbing, reflecting, vibrating
Pitch, volume
Sound

Name: _____   Date: _____

Rhymes and Rhythms Planning Guide

Directions: With your partner, conduct research about your science concept and record important words and/or rhythmic phrases you discover. Then brainstorm interesting rhymes and/or rhythms you may want to include in your poem. You also may record words and phrases about related science concepts to help you.

Science Concept	Rhyming Words and/or Rhythmic Phrases

Interesting Word Rhymes	Interesting Word Rhythms

   © Shell Education

Name: _____ Date: _____

My Science Concept Poem

Directions: Use the space to write and illustrate your science concept poem.

Concept
Poem
Illustration

Structured Poems

Model Lesson: Cinquain

Overview

The cinquain structure guides the development of a poem by inviting the writer to use a prescribed sequence of words, types of words, or syllables in each line. Students write cinquain poems as they note the patterns in the structure and reflect on scientific concepts and vocabulary.

Materials

- *Cinquain Examples* (page 129)
- *Word-Count Cinquain Planner* (page 130)
- *Parts of Speech Cinquain Planner* (page 131)
- *Syllables Cinquain Planner* (page 132)
- *Elements of Poetry* (page 97)
- *Poetry Craft Tips* (page 105)

Standards

Grades K–2

- Makes observations to provide evidence that heat can be produced in many ways
- Writes a poetic narrative
- Demonstrates understanding of word relationships and rhyme in writing

Grades 3–5

- Knows that heat is often produced as a by-product when one form of energy is converted to another form
- Produces clear and coherent writing appropriate to poetic form
- Demonstrates understanding of word relationships and rhyme in writing

Grades 6–8

- Knows that energy is a property of many substances (heat energy is in the disorderly motion of molecules and in radiation; chemical energy is in the arrangement of atoms; mechanical energy is in moving bodies or in elastically distorted shapes; electrical energy is in the attraction or repulsion between charges)
- Produces clear and coherent writing appropriate to poetic form
- Demonstrates understanding of language, word relationships, and rhyme in writing

Grades 9–12

- Discusses solutions for reducing the effects of human activities on the environment and biodiversity
- Produces clear and coherent writing in which the development, organization, and style are appropriate to task, purpose, and audience
- Demonstrates understanding of figurative language, word relationships, and nuances in word meanings

Structured Poems (cont.)

Preparation

Try writing a cinquain poem to experience working within the structures prescribed in the *Word-Count Cinquain Planner*, the *Parts of Speech Cinquain Planner*, and the *Syllables Cinquain Planner*. Reflect on the criteria of the poems that you found easiest to meet and those you found most challenging. Additional suggestions are provided in the Specific Grade-Level Ideas.

> "Both poetry and science seek to contain chaos through form, and through experimentation and manipulation, to arrive at new (and often complex) understandings or solutions to the conundrums and idiosyncrasies that plague our ever-evolving environment."
>
> —Sandra L. Faulkner and Abigail Cloud (2019, xxii)

Procedure

1. Display the *Cinquain Examples* activity sheet, or share cinquains of your own creation. Read the poems aloud to students, have students read along with you, or ask student volunteers to read the poems aloud. Then read the poems to students again, asking listeners to consider the rhythm, word choices, and mood and to identify how the poem brings a scientific idea to life.

2. Ask, "What do you notice about how these poems bring scientific ideas to life? What do you learn about each concept? How are these poems alike?" Allow time for students to identify ideas related to the number of lines, the number of words in each line, the types of words in each line, the scientific theme, and the shape of the poems.

3. As a class, select a scientific concept about which to write a class cinquain poem. Then collectively identify a term for the first line of the poem. Invite students to brainstorm additional words associated with this concept. Suggested terms and concepts to use for the first line of the poems are listed in the Specific Grade Level Ideas. You also can refer students to a science word wall if you have one in your classroom.

4. Display the *Word-Count Cinquain Planner*, the *Parts of Speech Cinquain Planner*, or the *Syllables Cinquain Planner*, whichever is most appropriate for students. As a class, work through ideas for the different lines of the class poem, drawing from the list of brainstormed words.

5. Divide the class into small groups and have each group create a cinquain poem, either by building on the ideas generated as a class or by creating a new poem on a different scientific topic. Circulate among the groups and use the Planning Questions to help students visualize images and use their senses. Note that these poem structures are not meant to be formulaic but rather provide structures to spark creativity. The cinquain structure prompts students to make careful choices about how best to represent ideas and distill their thinking.

6. Have each group read their cinquain poem aloud to the class. Use the Discussion Questions to debrief the activity.

Planning Questions

- What word will you choose to start your poem? What related word will you use for the last line?

- Close your eyes and think about your word. What do you see? What do you feel? What does this word remind you of? Which words on the list do you like best?

- What actions can you brainstorm that connect to your word? Which action words give new insights about the scientific ideas?

- What feelings do you associate with this scientific term?

Structured Poems (cont.)

Discussion Questions

▸ What choices did you make as you selected words and phrases for your poem?

▸ What did you learn from the poems read by other members of our class?

▸ What language was most compelling?

▸ How did the sound and rhythm of the poems help communicate meaning?

▸ What are the main ideas communicated about each topic?

▸ How does writing a poem compare to sharing ideas in essays or book chapters?

Specific Grade-Level Ideas

Grades K–2

It will be easiest for students to focus on the number of words in each line of a cinquain while using the *Word-Count Cinquain Planner* activity sheet.

Possible words for the first line include general terms describing heat (*hot, mixing, burning, rubbing, energy*), heat produced by burning (*fire, wood, coal, sun, light, ash*), or heat produced by rubbing things together (*friction, movement, hands, warm*). Students also may use particular ideas about heat that are relevant to them, such as a fireplace, a campfire, or a candle.

This strategy can be used to explore other scientific topics such as weather (*rain, snow, water cycle*), living organisms (*animal, plant, needs, ecosystem*), or energy (*sun, electricity, sound, light*).

Grades 3–5

Have students use the *Word-Count Cinquain Planner* or the *Parts of Speech Cinquain Planner* activity sheet. Possible words for the first line include ways that heat is produced when living organisms convert stored energy to motion (*breathe, run, swim, sprout, grow, bloom*), heat that is produced when machines convert stored energy to motion (*kinetic, engine, motor, turbine, noise, spark, gears*), heat that moves from one object to another by conduction (*transfer, flow, gradient, thermal, diffusion*), or properties associated with heat conductivity (*insulation, thermal, conductivity, coefficient, resistivity*).

This strategy can be used to explore other topics such as the water cycle, the composition of Earth, or plant structure and growth.

Grades 6–8

Have students use the *Syllables Cinquain Planner* activity sheet. Have students consider the concept of energy as a property of many substances, using *heat, mechanical, electrical,* or *chemical* for possible first lines.

Grades 9–12

Have students write a cinquain poem about the design process: *ask, imagine, plan, create, improve*. Students also could write a cinquain poem on the topic of environmental advocacy in response to viewing an environmental art installation online, such as the art from the GAIA collection or from artist Resa Blatman.

Cinquain Examples

Word-Count Cinquain

Hot
Fire, flames
Burning, crackling, glowing
Warmth from the hearth
Heat

Parts of Speech Cinquain

Mobile
Quickly moving
Rolling, rambling, rusting
Burning dirty fossil fuels
Auto

Syllables Cinquain

Turn, turn
Wind turbines move
Transferring energy
Transforming shaping people's lives
Whoosh, whoosh

Name: _____ Date: _____

Word-Count Cinquain Planner

Directions: Collect words about your topic of study. Then use the structure to create a meaningful cinquain poem. Experiment with different word choices.

Topic of my poem: _____

_____

Word collection: _____

_____

_____

My poem:

Title: _____

One word: _____

Two words: _____ _____

Three words: _____ _____ _____

Four words: _____ _____ _____ _____

One word: _____

Name: _____ Date: _____

Parts of Speech Cinquain Planner

Directions: Collect words about your topic of study. Then use the structure to create a meaningful cinquain poem. Experiment with different word choices.

Topic of my poem: _____

_____

Word collection: _____

_____

_____

My poem:

Title: _____

Adjectives: _____ _____

-*ing* words: _____ _____ _____

Phrase: _____ _____ _____ _____

Synonym for title word: _____

117846—Integrating the Arts in Science

Name: _____ Date: _____

Syllables Cinquain Planner

Directions: Collect words about your topic of study. Then use the structure to create a meaningful cinquain poem. Experiment with different word choices.

Topic of my poem: _____

_____

Word collection: _____

_____

_____

My poem:

Title: _____

Two syllables: _____ _____

Four syllables: _____ _____ _____ _____

Six syllables: _____ _____ _____ _____ _____ _____

Eight syllables: _____ _____ _____ _____ _____ _____ _____

Two syllables: _____ _____

MUSIC

Music

Understanding Music

Music has played a significant role in every culture since the beginning of time. Our favorite tunes are readily available to us given our ever-present smartphones, and music has become even more prevalent in our lives. But the question is, how can music be easily and effectively integrated into the curriculum? For some students, connecting with rhythm, beat, and melody provides individual access to learning. Any teacher who has created a cleanup song knows music can motivate children and help them make transitions from one activity to another. Recently, attention has been given to the benefits of integrating music in academic performance. It has been suggested that early music training develops language skills, spatial relations, and memory (Perret and Fox 2006). Music and the sciences have long been linked. From the sounds of birdsong to the physical characteristics of musical instruments that shape their particular tone and timbre, scientific concepts have helped us understand how sounds and music are created, shaped, and changed.

In the strategies described in this section, students explore scientific ideas alongside the basic elements of music and sound. Students engage in singing, playing, and composing music as well as making an instrument. The focus is on deepening scientific knowledge while experiencing the joy of creating music together in ways in which all students participate. Asking students to "listen up" is common in every classroom, but teaching students how to listen and what it means to really listen is often overlooked. The musical strategies provided here will focus on deepening knowledge of listening—which is a fundamental musical skill—as well as deepening knowledge of and skills in science. By implementing these musical strategies, students also will develop a deeper understanding of and skills in creating music. No previous musical training is needed for you or your students.

Integrating music into the science curriculum engages and motivates students. As students identify, apply, and generalize ideas to real-world situations, scientific concepts become meaningful and purposeful. Abstract ideas are connected to concrete models, and students' representational fluency deepens. The more avenues we provide for students to experience scientific concepts, the more likely we are to connect with the variable ways in which students learn.

Elements of Music

The most basic accepted definition of *music* is "organized/intentional sound and silence."

According to Jacobsen (1992) and Estrella (2019), the basic elements of music from a Western perspective include the following:

- **Pitch:** The highness and lowness on a musical scale

- **Harmony:** Notes of different pitches played at the same time

- **Melody:** How notes are put together in a sequence

- **Dynamics:** The loudness and quietness of composition (musical piece) and transitions between the two

- **Rhythm:** How time is controlled in music (beat, meter, tempo)

- **Timbre/tone color:** The sound quality of a note

- **Texture:** The number of layers in a composition (musical piece)

Music (cont.)

Strategies for Music

Found Sounds

Sounds are all around us; they are found when we attend to them or manipulate them. Think about the sound of light rain, the rustle of leaves, the wind in the trees, or the squeals of delight you hear near a playground. There is rhythm in these sounds. Composer R. Murray Schafer thinks about the world as a musical composition. He notes, "We must learn how to listen. It seems to be a habit we have forgotten. We must sensitize the ear to the miraculous world around us" (1992). What makes a sound musical rather than sounding like noise may depend on the listener, but it also is related to pitch, rhythm, tempo, and tone color or timbre. When students collect found sounds, they gain a new appreciation for what music is and develop careful listening skills. They also can better understand the environment from which sounds come. Students can put sounds together in interesting compositions, exploring environments and contexts from where stories unfold, as well as the power of onomatopoeia as language mirrors sounds. Louise Pascale notes, "Often, we describe things visually rather than auditorily. Students can describe the sounds they hear in a more vivid way (a loud sound can become an ear-piercing sound, brassy, shattering, etc.). This can build language" (personal communication, 2012). This strategy is an excellent way to prepare students for the soundscape strategy and is particularly conducive to teaching remotely. Sounds can be found anywhere and easily shared online or face-to-face.

Sampling

When a musical composition is sampled, a small portion of that music is taken and repurposed into a different song or piece to gain a new meaning. Made popular by the rise of electronic instruments and sound recorders, sampling is a major element in hip-hop and rap. It primarily involves reusing elements, or "samples," of audio or instrumentation from popular music or sound bites from the internet and television. A sample can be constructed as a loop or a rhythmic portion of something, or it can be the repetition of larger phrases in a music composition. Henry Jenkins notes in his text on media education in the twenty-first century, "Many of the forms of expression that are most important to American youths accent this sampling and remixing process, in part because digitalization makes it much easier to combine and repurpose media content than ever before" (2009, 32).

Chants

Chants involve the rhythmic repetition of sounds or words without a melody. Similar to rap, they are spoken to a variety of rhythms, pitches, and tempos. By combining varying dynamics (ranging from soft to loud), pitch (variations from high to low), tempos (speed), and even movement, students can create engaging chants that help them learn and remember information more easily. Chants can be created about any content topic, such as parts of speech, the steps in a life cycle, or the names of the continents. Chants also can be constructed by layering lines on top of each other that are then spoken simultaneously. An essential component of using chants as a musical strategy is to have the students add a movement to support each statement or phrase. This reinforces the lyrics by having students not only verbalize the lyrics but transfer the understanding of the words into their bodies.

Music *(cont.)*

Many chants are available online and are effective to use as examples, but it is critical that students create chants themselves. If they create the lyrics and the movements, they'll own the chant as "theirs," and they are much more likely to remember it.

> "Chants are useful because they draw on the power of rhymes and rhythm. They can help students make content material more engaging, informative, and memorable because once students become more engaged, they also learn at a much deeper level."
>
> —Lisa Ciecierski and William Bintz (2012)

Songwriting

When students sing, they create a deep connection with the melody, rhythm, and lyrics of a song. Writing songs about scientific concepts can make science topics more accessible while increasing students' engagement. Students can explore the development of scientific identities and deepen personal connections to and find relevance in science content (Ward et al. 2018). Although students might have the opportunity to sing in school, far less attention is given to challenging them to create their own songs as a strategy for directly connecting to and enhancing a particular content area. Songwriting invites students to become lyricists, and as they do, they become familiar not only with the importance of tone, rhythm, and tempo but with the power of rhythmic language to convey meaning. Educators can use music and songwriting integrated with science content to build understanding of topics. Students make meaning engaging in new approaches with vocabulary, explanations of science concepts, and making sense to build understanding. Songs can also support student's ability to remember core ideas in science (Governor, Hall, and Jackson 2013). Students can

begin by creating new lyrics to a familiar melody. Song lyrics, put to a rhythm and/or melody, help the brain remember information far beyond simply stating facts. And creating original lyrics prompts students to discuss, synthesize, and categorize curricular concepts. As they get more comfortable, students may choose to create original melodies and even score their written compositions.

Instrumentation

This strategy focuses on the instruments used within a composition. Students can investigate the ways in which sounds are made, explore the skills needed to play different instruments, compare the different sounds instruments can make, and analyze the effect of different instruments within a musical piece. They also can construct their own instruments and experiment with how choices in their construction affect the sound that is made. As noted by Jeanne Bamberger (2000), "The question 'I wonder why that happened?' becomes the basis for interrogation, reflection and experimenting, and thus eventually for new ideas" (33). Students apply their knowledge of the composition and characteristics of materials (strength, density, hardness, and flexibility) as they make their instruments.

> "Music gives a soul to the universe."
>
> —Plato

Found Sounds

Model Lesson: Noise on My Street

Overview

In this lesson, students listen to, gather, and categorize sounds in the school environment. They learn about dynamics, duration, and pitch, and they interpret how the sound is made. They perform music by re-creating the sounds through the creative use of materials and playing with the composition.

Materials

▸ *Sound Observation Chart* (page 142)

▸ *Sound Categories* (page 143)

▸ *Elements of Music* (page 135)

Standards

Grades K–2

▸ Makes observations to construct evidence-based learning opportunities

▸ Knows patterns in the natural world can be observed

▸ Demonstrates and explains reasons for personal choices of musical ideas

▸ Presents a final version of personal musical ideas

Grades 3–5

▸ Knows that scientists' explanations come partly from what they observe (evidence) and partly from how they interpret (inference)

▸ Knows that pitch is the highness or lowness of a sound

▸ Explains selected and organized musical ideas

▸ Describes connection of personally created music to expressive intent

Grades 6–8

▸ Knows that sound waves are reflected, absorbed, or transmitted through various materials.

▸ Applies scientific principles to design a method to gather, analyze, and interpret scientific data

▸ Explains how knowledge relates to personal choices and intent when creating and performing music

▸ Demonstrates relationship between music and another discipline

Grades 9–12

▸ Plans and conducts an investigation to gather scientific evidence

▸ Uses technology and mathematics to plan and conduct an investigation to gather scientific evidence

▸ Demonstrates how sounds and musical ideas can represent concepts or texts

Found Sounds (cont.)

Preparation

Select a school location where students will be able to find many sounds, such as the playground, sports field, cafeteria, or another classroom. Practice the lesson on your own so you get a sense of what it feels like and what questions might arise.

Gather everyday materials found in the classroom or the natural environment, such as dried leaves, small rocks, paper, rulers, pencils, small pieces of bubble wrap, or water bottles. You could also choose to have students bring in objects that they might use to make sound (nothing electric). Additional suggestions are provided in the Specific Grade-Level Ideas.

Procedure

1. Divide the class into groups of three or four students and distribute the *Sound Observation Chart* to each group. Explain to students that they will be going to a location to listen to and observe sounds. Review the *Sound Observation Chart* activity sheet with students. Tell them they should find at least eight sounds during their observation and describe and note each sound on the *Sound Observation Chart* activity sheet.

2. Take students to the chosen location and allow them approximately 15 minutes to work together to gather sounds and note them on the *Sound Observation Chart* activity sheet.

3. After returning to the classroom, have students share and compare their sound observations. Ask students to describe the qualities of the sounds they heard (for example, the most common types of sounds, high or low sounds, quiet or loud sounds).

4. Introduce students to the following music vocabulary:

   - *duration*: the length of time a sound is heard
   - *dynamic*: variations of volume or loudness
   - *form*: repetition, contrast, variation
   - *pitch*: high or low sounds
   - *texture*: layers of sound
   - *timbre*: characteristics of the sound itself

5. Ask students to name various sounds they found with respect to the *pitch* (high or low), the *duration* (short or long), and the *dynamic* (soft or loud) of the sound. Distribute the *Sound Categories* activity sheet to each group and have students categorize their sounds.

6. Provide small groups with items to explore such as small pieces of bubble wrap (might sound like a fire crackling); a metal water bottle with a hard object (might sound like a bell) or a hammer; shaking a water bottle (depending on how fast you shake it, can sound like a bubbling brook or water lapping on the shore). Have students "play" the objects as instruments, one a time, while the others in the group listen carefully to each one, closing their eyes and discovering how each sound can conjure up an image of something else once the focus is on listening.

7. Have each student choose one sound from their group's observations. Tell students to practice re-creating their chosen sound using the provided items.

Found Sounds *(cont.)*

8. Allow time for students to experiment and make found sounds with different objects and combinations of objects to match the sounds from their observation charts. Explain to students that everyone in the group works together as a team to make the most accurate sounds possible. To test the sounds for accuracy, one person in the group might play the found sound that the group has chosen to re-create a sound while the rest of the group listens to test to see how accurate the sound really is. If it's not quite right, they all can brainstorm how to improve the sound. Maybe it takes two or three people to accurately make the sound. Encourage the listeners to close their eyes while the other group member(s) make the sound. Explain that once their eyes are closed, it is easier to envision the sounds as representative of something else. Listeners can then make careful edits. Remind students that a major part of this process is to experiment, use creative thinking skills, and feel free to keep editing until it is just perfect.

9. Tell student groups to work together to create a composition using their individual sounds. Explain that sounds can be made one after the other or overlapped (texture). Students can experiment with musical form, playing with repetition, contrast, and variation. Students should pay attention to pitch, duration, and dynamic as they decide how to arrange the sounds. Have each group perform their composition for the class. Use the Discussion Questions to debrief.

Discussion Questions

▸ What do you think caused the found sounds? How do you know?

▸ What did you notice about pitch, duration, and dynamic in the compositions?

▸ What artistic choices did you make when creating your compositions?

▸ What worked well? What might you change next time?

"To test for sound accuracy, one person(s) creates the sound(s) while the others, with their eyes closed, carefully listen for preciseness. Adjustments may then need to be made. The crucial component in this process is experimentation and editing. It's almost impossible to create accurate sounds on the first try. Working out the problems as a team makes the challenge much more fun."

—Dr. Louise Pascale
(personal communication, 2021)

"Simply listen to the sounds without looking at the source. Imagine you are creating sound effects for radio or a movie."

—Dr. Louise Pascale
(personal communication, 2021)

Found Sounds (cont.)

Specific Grade-Level Ideas

Grades K–2

Before collecting found sounds, spend time with students making loud sounds, soft sounds, high sounds, and low sounds. Students should collect just one or two sounds. Once sounds have been collected, have students identify where their sounds came from and have them pretend they are the source of the sound. This may help them more easily re-create the sound.

Students also can explore bird and animal sounds, talk about how animals and birds interrelate, and look at ecology rather than acoustics.

Grades 3–5

Students can find more sounds, and perhaps each student can perform one sound that is high and one sound that is low. Their performance can be a little longer with a few more sounds. Extend this activity by having students use found objects to reproduce the sounds. Explain that sounds are vibrations and that pitch depends on the frequency of the vibrations.

Students also can explore how scientists use data collection in their work. They can use the strategy to explore how scientists collect samples, take measurements, and observe the natural world. Have them conduct a keyword search for "research stations in Antarctica" to provide them with a case study of scientific data collection at one of the research stations.

Grades 6–8

Have students gather sounds in the field with their cell phones or other recording software. When they return to the classroom, have them listen to their recordings and note the sounds on the *Sound Observation Chart* activity sheet.

Students can work together to create a longer and more nuanced composition, and they can give it a name.

Students also can explore how scientists use tools to extend their senses. For example, how do microscopes, binoculars, magnifying glasses, or telescopes allow scientists to observe things they ordinarily could not see?

Grades 9–12

Have students add a column to the *Sound Observation Chart* titled "Natural or Human-made." As students gather sounds in their charts, they can evaluate whether the sound occurs naturally or is human made. At the end, students can make generalizations about the quantity of natural versus human-made sounds and what that might mean for the specific setting where students are making their observations (for example, a city's downtown area or a more rural area).

Name: _____ Date: _____

Sound Observation Chart

Directions: Use this chart to document the sounds you find during your sound exploration.

Group name: _____

Sound Name	Pitch (high to low)	Duration (how long)	Dynamic (loud to quiet)	Sound Source

Found Sounds

Name: _____ Date: _____

Sound Categories

Directions: List the sounds you collected in the categories. Categorize each sound according to pitch, duration, and dynamic.

Pitch		
low	medium	high

Duration		
short	medium	long

Dynamic		
quiet	medium	loud

Sampling

Model Lesson: The Human Weather Sampler

Overview

In this lesson, students read and listen to local weather reports by the National Weather Service (NWS) and the National Oceanic and Atmospheric Administration (NOAA). They "sample" portions of a given section by listening to and repeating phrases they hear. Students perform a short piece based on the weather patterns for that day, each taking turns playing the "human sampler."

Materials

- *Sampling and Sound* (page 148)
- *Elements of Music* (page 135)
- examples of sampled songs
- index cards and pens or pencils
- "sampling hat"

Standards

Grades K–2

- Uses and shares observations of local weather conditions to describe patterns over time
- Demonstrates knowledge of music concepts and contrasts
- Demonstrates and describes music's expressive qualities

Grades 3–5

- Describes typical weather conditions expected during a particular season
- Demonstrates understanding of structure and elements of music
- Demonstrates and describes how intent is conveyed through expressive qualities of music

Grades 6–8

- Describes how patterns of atmospheric and oceanic circulation determine regional climates
- Demonstrates and describes how intent is conveyed through expressive qualities of music
- Demonstrates relationship between music and another discipline

Grades 9–12

- Understands that most scientists and engineers work in teams to apply scientific ideas to design, test, and refine their work
- Demonstrates and describes how intent is conveyed through expressive qualities of music
- Demonstrates the relationship between music and another discipline

Sampling *(cont.)*

Preparation

Prior to the lesson, have students listen to a weather forecast for homework and write key phrases about the weather they hear. Or, complete this activity as a class prior to completing the lesson.

Visit the National Weather Service website (**forecast.weather.gov**) and enter your zip code. Scroll down to "Additional Forecasts and Information" and click on "Forecast Discussion." Then print the Forecast Discussion. (*Note*: Clicking the hyperlinked words in the Forecast Discussion will take you to the entry for each word in the National Weather Service glossary.)

Select examples of sampled songs to share with students. One well-known example uses barking dogs to sing "Jingle Bells." An internet search for "Jingle Bell Dogs" will yield many versions to sample.

Find or make a distinctive and easy-to-wear "sampling hat" or other engaging device to designate the student who is directing the group by "playing" the samples. Additional suggestions are provided in the Specific Grade-Level Ideas.

Procedure

1. Ask students to share the weather-related phrases they heard in a weather forecast. Record these phrases for students to refer to throughout the lesson.

2. Read students the current National Weather Service Forecast Discussion for your region. When reading a Forecast Discussion from the National Weather Service website, the hyperlinked vocabulary will direct you to a glossary with a definition of the term. Be sure to emphasize this vocabulary.

3. Ask students if they hear any phrases from the Forecast Discussion that they heard in the weather forecast they listened to for homework. Ask them if there is any difference between this report and the report they heard. Add any new weather words or phrases to the recorded list.

4. Ask students to look at the underlined (or hyperlinked) words from the Forecast Discussion and think of a type of sound that weather might make that they could re-create with their bodies or voices. Distribute the *Sampling and Sound* activity sheet and have students complete the chart. Have them demonstrate their ideas with partners.

5. Ask students if they know what *sampling* is. Explain that sampling is the taking of small portions of sound or music and mixing it with other sounds in a song. If desired, play examples of sampled songs for students.

6. Divide the class into groups of six to eight. Ask groups to select a short phrase from the weather forecast they heard, the Forecast Discussion, or a weather sound; make sure each student has a weather "sample" to practice aloud. Students may use the *Sampling and Sound* activity sheet to guide them through this process.

7. Have students line up with their groups. Put on the "sampling hat." Tell students that whoever wears the "sampling hat" plays the different "weather samples." Select one of the groups, and tell the group that when you point to a student in the group, that person will "play" their "sample" (i.e., they will make their selected weather sound). Each student represents only one sound. Meanwhile, have the rest of the students clap to a steady and slow beat. Once the beat is established, point to different students in the group to "play" their samples. Experiment with making a sampled song with each group.

Sampling *(cont.)*

8. When students are comfortable with the process, tell them that when you point lower, they should make their sound lower and slower. When you point higher, they should make their sound higher and faster. Practice with each group.

9. Let students take turns wearing the "sampling hat" and "playing" the samples to create unique compositions.

10. Use the Discussion Questions to debrief the activity.

Discussion Questions

▶ What did you learn about the weather from listening to a weather forecast?

▶ What weather words and phrases help describe weather patterns in specific ways?

▶ How did hearing the "weather samples" add to your weather vocabulary?

▶ What are your favorite weather phrases? Why? What do they mean?

Sampling (cont.)

Specific Grade-Level Ideas

Grades K–2

Instead of reading a Forecast Discussion, read aloud a weather report from the National Weather Service website and ask students what they think the report means. Give students key sounds and phrases to repeat, and rather than working in small groups, work as a whole class. Do this over a period of a week until students have internalized the basic weather vocabulary and concepts. You can also explore the sounds of weather by listening to recordings of weather sounds and recreating them.

Grades 3–5

As an extension, have students find the definitions of the vocabulary words the National Weather Service uses and use those words in a weather report they invent.

This strategy can be used to explore vocabulary from any area of science.

Grades 6–8

Have students further develop their own music compositions, using electronic recording software such as GarageBand or Stagelight. Students can easily sample weather words or phrases and play them back.

This strategy also can be used to explore vocabulary used in geology or Earth science, and students can research the meaning of the vocabulary terms. If the technology to record audio is not available, have students work in groups of five or six to create the "Human Looper" by repeating various words in groups.

Grades 9–12

Take advantage of the audio resources that NASA offers. There are many student and teacher resources on the NASA website. The Radio JOVE Project—an educational program designed for students to learn about radio astronomy—is very interesting, and you can use the audio from the Space Transportation System (STS) missions to create sampling compositions based on NASA audio resources. Audacity is a free open source audio editor that students can use to layer their compositions.

Sampling and Sound

Directions: Complete the chart to help you think of ways to re-create the sounds weather can make.

Sampling

Key vocabulary words from the weather forecast or Forecast Discussion	Sounds weather can make	Ways I can re-create the sound with my body or voice

Chants

Model Lesson: The Phyla of Life on Earth

Overview

Chanting is a musical strategy that can help students learn taxonomies in science. Using pitch and rhythm, students create musical compositions that help them learn various phrases and sentences common to scientific inquiry. In this lesson, students use chanting to learn about taxonomy and the scientific classification systems for living creatures.

Materials

- large roll of paper
- painter's tape (that will stick and restick)
- *Tree of Life* (page 153)
- poster board
- thick, dark markers
- *Elements of Music* (page 135)

Standards

Grades K–2

- Uses observations to describe similarities and differences in the appearance and behavior of plants and animals
- Demonstrates knowledge of music concepts and contrasts
- Demonstrates and describes music's expressive qualities

Grades 3–5

- Analyzes and interprets data to provide evidence that plants and animals can be grouped based on shared characteristics
- Demonstrates understanding of structure and elements of music
- Demonstrates and describes how intent is conveyed through expressive qualities of music

Grades 6–8

- Analyzes and interprets data to provide evidence that plants and animals can be grouped based on shared characteristics
- Demonstrates and describes how intent is conveyed through expressive qualities of music
- Demonstrates the relationship between music and another discipline

Grades 9–12

- Constructs an explanation based on evidence for how natural selection leads to adaptation of populations
- Demonstrates and describes how intent is conveyed through expressive qualities of music
- Demonstrates the relationship between music and another discipline

Chants (cont.)

Preparation

Prior to the lesson, have students find pictures of living creatures and bring them to class. These can be drawn, printed online, or cut out from magazines. Additional suggestions are provided in the Specific Grade-Level Ideas.

Procedure

1. Lay a large sheet of paper on the floor and invite students to sit around it, bringing with them the images of living creatures they brought to class. Have students lay their images on the large paper. Talk about the different characteristics that living creatures share, and work together to sort and categorize the images into different groups. Encourage students to consider several kinds of grouping strategies.

2. Introduce students to the concept of taxonomy and classification, and decide as a class on one particular way of classifying the life forms according to the characteristics students identified. Have students sort the images into clearly defined groups on the large paper and tape the images in place with painter's tape.

3. Talk with students about the classification system of Kingdom-Phylum-Subphylum-Class-Order-Family-Genus-Species. Distribute the *Tree of Life* activity sheet and review it with students. Talk about shared characteristics, and explain that the further down the Tree of Life they go, the fewer and fewer shared characteristics are found in each group.

4. Return to the initial grouping of the images students sorted. Ask students how their classification system is different from the Tree of Life and how it is similar. Assist students in grouping the images by kingdom or phylum.

5. Tell students that they will create chants about the Tree of Life classification system. Explain that in a chant, each line is sung or spoken by a group with a particular rhythmic pattern and pitch (high or low vocal tone). Introduce the musical term *ostinato* as a repetition of similar rhythmic patterns and tones.

6. As a class, do the simple chant "Kingdom-Phylum-Subphylum-Class-Order-Family-Genus-Species." Introduce students to the term *pitch* (highness or lowness of a tone). Ask students to use a low voice for Kingdom, and as each word is chanted, have them use a slightly higher voice until they get to Species. At the end, have students clap three times. If desired, have students crouch low on the floor, slowly moving higher as their voices get higher as well. Then, have students repeat the chant in reverse from high voice to low voice until they return to Kingdom. Students should again clap three times.

7. Introduce students to the concept of *rhythm* (repeating beat). Have students repeat the chant quickly and then slowly. Introduce students to the term *dynamics* (softness or loudness). Then have them do the chant loudly and then softly. Finally, introduce students to the term *duration* (length of a sound or note) and have them repeat the chant by saying each word quickly and then drawing the words out.

8. Divide the class into groups of four or five. Assign each group a different kingdom classification: *Plantae*, *Animalia*, *Fungi*, *Protista*, and *Moneran*, which includes *Eubacteria* and *Archaebacteria*. Have students choose an organism in their assigned kingdom and research the names for the phylum, subphylum, class, order, family, genus, and species. Students will use these series of names for their chants.

Chants *(cont.)*

9. Give each group a sheet of poster board and a thick, dark marker. Have each group prepare a chant based on the classification of their species and write it on the poster board. Ask students to practice using various elements of rhythm, pitch, and dynamics of sound. Circulate among the groups and use the Planning Questions to help students plan their chants.

10. Provide time for groups to rehearse their chants.

11. Bring the class together as a whole. Ask each group the name of their species, and then ask each group to display their poster and perform their chant. Use the Discussion Questions to debrief the activity.

Planning Questions

‣ What pitch will you use?

‣ What dynamics will you use?

‣ What rhythms are suggested by the words in your line?

‣ What other sound effects might you add to give your phrase more interest (clapping, stomping, slapping the desk, and so forth)?

‣ What gestures can you add to emphasize your tempo (slow, curved motions or quick, jagged moves)?

Discussion Questions

‣ What did you learn about the species you chose?

‣ How was it different from other species in its genus or family?

‣ Did anything surprise you in the sound of the names of the different classifications?

‣ Describe the musical aspects of your chant (beat, dynamics, pitch, duration).

‣ Why might a scientist want to classify living creatures?

‣ What are some other ideas you could use to make your chants more interesting?

‣ What artistic choices did you make in the creation of your chant?

Chants (cont.)

Specific Grade-Level Ideas

Grades K–2

Talk with students about what living creatures have in common and what is different. As a group, create a chant based on students' ideas.

This strategy can be used to help students memorize other science concepts, such as the structure and function of organisms.

Grades 3–5

Give students a broad overview of the kingdoms as a classification system, and then ask them which kingdom they think the organism in their picture belongs to. Have students discuss which of the various animals or plants share characteristics and which are different.

Divide the class into pairs and have each pair choose one of the images of living creatures. Have each pair create a short chant about their creature and its characteristics and perform it for the class. Invite students to include found sounds or instruments to add musical interest.

Grades 6–8

Students can delve deeper into the concept of biodiversity and how it is captured and categorized. This strategy also can be used to help students memorize other science concepts, such as characteristics of Earth's system—core, mantle, lithosphere, hydrosphere, and atmosphere. Ask students to teach the class their chants with movement and sound.

Grades 9–12

Have students create chants around natural selection and the process of adaptation over time, about the impact of nutrition on cells in the body, or ways to support healthy living—both physical and mental. Challenge students to add movement to emphasize key ideas.

Tree of Life

Animal (Animalia)

Plant (Plantae)

Kingdom

Phylum

Subphylum

Class

Order

Family

Genus

Species

Songwriting

Model Lesson: Science Songs

Overview

Creating original lyrics to familiar melodies encourages students to explore new learning or demonstrate what they have learned. In this lesson, students demonstrate their knowledge at the end of a unit of study by writing new lyrics to an original song. Depending on the grade level, groups of students can write songs or the whole class can work together to create them.

Materials

- list of familiar melodies to be used for songwriting activity
- *Lyric Brainstorming Guide* (page 157)
- *Songwriting Planner* (page 158)
- *Elements of Music* (page 135)

Standards

Grades K–2

- Describes what happens when objects made of different materials are placed in the path of a beam of light and how objects in darkness can be seen only when illuminated
- Demonstrates how a specific music concept (melody) is used for a specific purpose
- Demonstrates and explains reasons for personal choices of musical ideas

Grades 3–5

- Describes how plants and animals have traits inherited from parents and that variation of these traits exists in a group of similar organisms
- Explains how responses to music are informed by the structure and elements of music, such as melody
- Describes the connection of personally created music to expressive intent

Grades 6–8

- Describes how sounds waves are reflected, absorbed, or transmitted through various materials
- Explains how responses to music are informed by the structure and elements of music, such as melody

Grades 9–12

- Describes how the structure of DNA determines the structure of proteins, which carry out the essential functions of life through systems of specialized cells
- Explains how responses to music are informed by the structure and elements of music, such as melody

Songwriting (cont.)

Preparation

This model lesson is written as a culminating activity, representing the knowledge gleaned from research about a selected topic/unit of study. Melodies used for the song lyrics can be familiar tunes such as "Twinkle, Twinkle Little Star." However, we all have different "familiar" tunes based on our cultural background and experiences. Be sure to encourage learners to use songs that are familiar to them. Additional suggestions are provided in the Specific Grade-Level Ideas.

There are websites that outline how to write a song, which may be helpful for you to review prior to teaching this strategy. Check out the resources at the Musical Futures website, for example (**www.musicalfutures.org/resource-type/songwriting-resources**).

Procedure

1. Tell students that as a culminating activity of their research/unit of study, they will write a song to share what they have learned.

2. Introduce or review the terms *melody, lyric, chorus,* and *verse*. Discuss how the chorus in the song reveals the main idea and the verses provide details. Explain to students that songwriting always includes a topic, a melody, a chorus/verses, and a purpose.

3. Display a list of songs that everyone is likely to know or could learn, such as "Old MacDonald Had a Farm," "Mary Had a Little Lamb," and "The Ants Go Marching." Consider including melodies from different cultural traditions as well. Be mindful that often songs have a chorus, which contains the main idea, and the verses of the song contain the details.

4. Distribute *Lyric Brainstorming Guide*. Have students complete the *Lyric Brainstorming Guide* to develop a rhyming structure for their lyrics, brainstorming potential words that rhyme with the word ending each line.

5. Distribute *Songwriting Planner*. Have students use the planning form to plan out an original song, with a known melody, and lyrics and a chorus.

6. Provide students time to share their songs with the class.

7. Use the Discussion Questions to talk with students about using the process of songwriting as a strategy for better understanding of a topic.

Discussion Questions

▸ How did you decide what information to include in your lyrics?

▸ What were the challenges of songwriting?

▸ How did songwriting help you deepen your understanding of the subject?

▸ What choices did you have to make when creating the lyrics and chorus to make the song work with the melody?

Songwriting *(cont.)*

Specific Grade-Level Ideas

Grades K–2

Students can write lyrics about the characteristics of light waves, including how light travels, how the availability of light lets us see objects, as well as how light can pass through some materials and not others or how light creates shadows.

Grades 6–8

Instruct students to write songs to describe the properties of sound waves, how they interact with matter, and how they can be used to send digital information.

Grades 3–5

Students can write lyrics about the similarities and differences in the life cycle of different organisms, their inherited traits, and how the environment affects the traits that organisms can develop.

Grades 9–12

Invite students to write songs about DNA and its importance to the function of life or the workings of the solar system, including details about the life of the sun, the composition of stars, and their movement and life span.

"In science class I wrote a song to the tune 'Jingle Bells.' While I was writing it I had to think about all the concepts involved and figure out how to make them rhyme. I could hear the rhyme and tune and picture the concepts in my mind. The most important thing is this: I had to think about, work with and write about the concepts. I didn't memorize them. I really learned them. I still remember them years later."

—Lisa Ciecierski and William Bintz (2012)

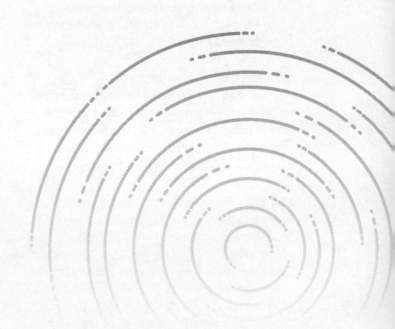

Name: _____ Date: _____

Lyric Brainstorming Guide

Directions: Use this chart to plan your song lyrics.

Main Idea	
Ideas about the Topic of Study	**Melody Ideas**
	• "Twinkle, Twinkle, Little Star" • "Skip to My Lou" • "Bingo" • "This Land Is Your Land" • "You Are My Sunshine" • "If You're Happy and You Know It" • "Row, Row, Row Your Boat" • "Yellow Submarine" List your own ideas below:
Lyric Ideas for Verses	**Potential Rhymes**

Name: _____ Date: _____

Songwriting Planner

Directions: Use this chart to plan your song structure.

Title of Song _____

Chorus (important ideas about the subject)

```
┌─────────────────────────────────────────────────────────┐
│                                                           │
│                                                           │
│                                                           │
│                                                           │
│                                                           │
│                                                           │
│                                                           │
│                                                           │
└─────────────────────────────────────────────────────────┘
```

Verse (details about the subject)

```
┌─────────────────────────────────────────────────────────┐
│                                                           │
│                                                           │
│                                                           │
│                                                           │
│                                                           │
│                                                           │
│                                                           │
└─────────────────────────────────────────────────────────┘
```

Instrumentation

Model Lesson: The "Don't Throw It Away" Band

Overview

In this strategy, students learn about the properties of sound as they design and build musical instruments from recycled materials. They research the acoustic properties of the instrument to find out why it makes a specific kind of sound. Then, they give their instrument a name based on what they have learned about its sound properties.

Materials

- clean objects from home that would otherwise have been discarded
- video samples of recycled instruments
- *Instrument Design* (page 163)
- craft materials, such as scissors, tape, glue, rubber bands, yarn, or wire
- *Elements of Music* (page 135)

Standards

Grades K–2

- Plans and conducts investigations to provide evidence that vibrating materials can make sound
- Demonstrates and explains reasons for personal choices of musical ideas
- Presents a final version of personal musical ideas

Grades 3–5

- Develops a model for sound waves that prove the pitch of a sound depends on the frequency of the vibration producing it
- Demonstrates and explains reasons for personal choices of musical ideas
- Describes the connection between personally created music and expressive intent

Grades 6–8

- Develops a model of sound waves to describe patterns in terms of amplitude and wavelength and to show that waves can cause objects to move
- Explains how knowledge relates to personal choices and intent when creating and performing music
- Demonstrates the relationship between music and another discipline

Grades 9–12

- Explains relationships among the frequency, wavelength, and speed of waves
- Demonstrates how sounds and musical ideas can represent concepts or texts

Instrumentation (cont.)

Preparation

Have students bring in three to four objects from home that would otherwise have been thrown away, such as small cardboard boxes, bottle caps, milk jugs, soda bottles, empty toilet paper or paper towel rolls, tin cans, and so on. Tell students that the items must be clean and that cans must not have sharp edges. Conduct an internet search for videos of "recycled instruments" and select videos of people playing recycled instruments to share with students. Also conduct a keyword search for "instrument families" to familiarize yourself with the differences between wind, percussion, and string instruments. For younger students, it may be helpful to also explore "The Young Person's Guide to the Orchestra." Additional suggestions are provided in the Specific Grade-Level Ideas.

Procedure

1. Gather all the objects students brought in from home in one place. Ask students if they know what usually happens to these used objects in their community. Talk about the differences between reusing and recycling objects. Discuss the materials the objects are made from. Tell students they are going to transform these objects into musical instruments.

2. Share videos of recycled instruments and ask students to listen carefully to the sounds. Ask them how they think the instruments make the sounds.

3. Ask students what they know about the differences between wind instruments, percussion instruments, and string instruments. Discuss vibration and describe how a sound wave works and how the sound reaches the ear.

4. Divide the class into groups of three or four students, and invite them to imagine they are a band that will make its own instruments. Explain that each of them will design a wind instrument, a string instrument, or a percussion instrument, or they can make an instrument that can be played in more than one way. Distribute the *Instrument Design* activity sheet and direct students to look over the available objects, using the activity sheet to help them design an instrument.

5. Have each group present their instrument designs to the class. Ask them to describe the sounds they think their instruments will make and why. They also can talk about how they think the instruments will work together as a band.

6. Provide students with craft supplies to create their instruments using the discarded objects according to their designs.

7. Invite students to play their instruments and listen carefully to the sounds they make. Have them write a short description of the properties of the sound their instruments make (dynamic, pitch, duration, and so on). Ask: "How high is it? How low is it? Is it loud or soft? Is it a long, sustained sound or a short, staccato sound?"

8. Talk with students about how to draw a sound wave that represents the properties of the sound their instrument makes. Share images of sound waves and compare characteristics of sound waves to characteristics of various sounds. Based on these observations, have students create visual inferences of what sound waves might look like for their instrument. Discuss how the sounds are different and why. Based on the sound properties of their instruments, ask students to name their instruments.

Instrumentation *(cont.)*

9. Have each band work together to create a short composition using their instruments. Provide time for practice.

10. Have each band perform their composition for the class and present their instruments and sound wave drawings. Use the Discussion Questions to debrief.

Discussion Questions

- How is the sound of a percussion instrument different from a wind instrument or a string instrument?

- How different was the sound of your own instrument from what you expected?

- What were the different sound properties of the different kinds of instruments?

- How did the instruments' materials make a difference in the way they sounded?

- What did you discover about how the different sounds in the band worked together?

"In addition to providing opportunities for personal connection to science, music offers a new entry point into science concepts and discourses."

—Gregory J. Crowther et al. (2016)

Instrumentation (cont.)

Specific Grade-Level Ideas

Grades K–2

Have students play with materials, such as rustling paper, to investigate the range of sounds they can make. You can give students specific instructions to build various kinds of instruments. Provide more supplementary materials, such as rubber bands and waxed paper, and make the instruments fairly simple to put together. Have students first play their completed instruments individually and then play together, focusing on rhythm as a means of performing. Students also could build instruments in pairs and take turns playing different kinds of instruments.

This strategy also can be used to develop instruments to investigate and replicate sounds in nature, such as water and wind, or other kinds of sounds related to animals.

Grades 3–5

Students can expand their knowledge about sound, vibration, the difference between high and low sounds, and how sounds change in relation to the materials used. Help students identify materials that can be used to accomplish a design through specific properties of shape, flexibility, and so on. Have students describe what makes a material appropriate for the design task at hand. When students create music as a group, have them focus on rhythm and pitch as a means of performing.

Grades 6–8

Students can go deeper into the intricacies of acoustics and sound waves. They also can consider the context and space and how sound waves bounce or are absorbed. This strategy also could be used to investigate the relationships between sounds. For example, students can replicate and play the sounds of a particular context, such as a specific ecosystem, or students could investigate structures and properties of matter.

Grades 9–12

Have students use this strategy in a study on the physics of vibration. Students can identify the kind of sound wave their instrument produces by using an oscilloscope. If you don't have an oscilloscope, conduct an internet search for "virtual oscilloscope" to find software that simulates an oscilloscope so students can see the sound wave. There are also apps, such as Soundbeam, that simulate an oscilloscope.

Ask students what instruments they play and if they play in a band, and use this as an opportunity to discuss the materials used in creating their instruments. Have them compare their instruments with examples of instruments from different cultures in their material and design choices.

Name: _____ Date: _____

Instrument Design

Directions: Think about the instrument you would like to create, then answer the questions.

---

1. What materials will you use to create your instrument?

_____

_____

2. How do you play your instrument?

_____

_____

3. Is it a string, percussion, or wind instrument, or a combination of these?

_____

4. What kind of sound do you expect it to make?

_____

_____

5. What kind of sound wave will your instrument make?

_____

Sketch the design of your instrument.	Sketch how your instrument is played.

Visual Arts

Visual Arts

Understanding Visual Arts

We are bombarded with images on a daily basis, and though we have become more skilled at reading the nontextual representation of ideas, our visual-literacy abilities need to develop further. Why, then, is education so often text-based? Working with images can provide opportunities for students to observe, notice details, and make meaning. Visual work can communicate nuances that words cannot. In this section, we explore how students can use visual art as a language that is more unstructured than text.

Particular to visual arts is hands-on work with various materials. Visual artists use their art in many ways—to create narratives, observe, explore patterns, translate, represent, and juxtapose ideas using visual communication. Using the elements of art—line, form, shape, color, texture, and pattern—students can investigate and create visual representations of ideas. They also can create images as a way to tell what they know.

Integrating the visual arts helps students see and express scientific principles visually. Incorporating visual imagery into your science lessons, as in any other academic content area, can help make scientific concepts more tangible, accessible, and engaging (Dacey and Lynch 2007). When students process visual information as well as verbal, they are using different parts of the brain. Allan Paivio suggests that learning can be expanded by the inclusion of visual imagery, allowing students what he termed "dual coding" (as cited in Reed 2010). All curricular areas have visual aspects, so providing students with the opportunity to work with multiple representations of content is easy to incorporate and will give students new ways to engage in and access ideas related to science.

Elements of Visual Art

The elements of visual art were informed by a review of the field, including the J. Paul Getty Museum (Getty, n.d.-a), the Institute for Arts Integration and STEAM (Riley 2017), and the Kennedy Center (Glatstein 2019).

- **Line:** A mark made by the path of a point moving in space; lines can be horizontal, vertical, or diagonal; they can vary in width, direction, and length

- **Shape:** A closed line; shapes can be geometric, often made up of straight edges, or they can be organic and made up of irregular, free-form edges; shapes are flat and can be a defined length and width

- **Color:** The response of the eyes to different wavelengths of light reflecting off objects; color can be defined by any of its three properties: hue (or name, such as red, blue, or green), intensity, and value

- **Form:** A three-dimensional shape that can be expressed by length, width, and depth

- **Texture:** The quality of a surface that can be seen and felt (rough, smooth, bumpy, and so on); texture can be real or implied, meaning that a surface can have a physical texture or visually appear to have a texture even though the surface is flat

- **Value:** The lightness or darkness of a color

- **Space:** The area between, around, above, below, or within objects; space can be defined as negative (such as the emptiness of holes) or positive; space also describes depth, or the illusion (idea) of depth

Visual Arts (cont.)

Principles of Design

These are informed by the J. Paul Getty Museum (Getty, n.d.-b), the Institute for Arts Integration and STEAM (Riley 2017), the Kennedy Center (Glatstein 2019), and PBS Learning Media (KET, 2014).

- **Balance**: Arrangement of art elements with attention to visual weight. Symmetrically balanced artworks feel stable; asymmetrically balanced artworks can create a feeling of instability or movement.

- **Movement**: An artwork can be composed suggesting a sense of action. The elements of art can be intentionally placed in ways that guide the viewer's eyes around the work.

- **Repetition**: Applying art elements so that the same element(s) are used again and again; repeating elements in a predictable way creates pattern.

- **Proportion**: Size relationship between objects or elements in an artwork.

- **Emphasis**: The part of the artwork that stands out in an eye-catching way; the center of interest.

- **Contrast**: The juxtaposition of elements in an artwork showing differences that make them stand out from each other; many things can be in contrast to each other, including colors, shapes, or textures.

- **Unity**: The use of elements of art to create harmony in a composition.

- **Variety**: Combining art elements in ways to create visual interest.

Strategies for Visual Arts

Visual Narrative

In this strategy, students create and arrange images in sequence to tell a story or create a narrative. The story can be told through images alone, or the pictures can interact with text.

Students' understanding of curricular content is enhanced as they create visual narratives that demonstrate or apply their learning. Often, creating a visual narrative makes it easier for students to grasp connections and clarify their thinking, which they can then translate into text. Students can illustrate historical concepts, translating their understanding into visual form. Through the visual arts, students can create imagery that represents patterns and visually captures cycles of change and growth that occurred over time.

Visual narratives can culminate in the creation of simple books, digital image essays, magazines, storyboards, comics, and other formats that are easy to make and give students the opportunity to compose content and apply and articulate their knowledge in new ways. Teaching artist and researcher Wendy Strauch-Nelson notes that students "seemed drawn to the complementary relationship between the linear style of words and the layered nature of images" (2011, 9).

Visual Experimentation

Experimentation is one of the key building blocks of visual art. Artists work with multiple ideas and materials with an element of free play that gives them the opportunity to investigate and discover ways in which materials can interact with each other. In her research on arts organizations, Shirley Brice-Heath discusses the language used by artists and students as they talk about "What if?" "How about" and "Could we try this?" types of questioning (1999). By playing with materials to explore "what if," students can develop imaginative solutions to artistic problems. Science and engineering require manipulating materials to see how they function. Art invites students to apply the knowledge gleaned from experimentation in a playful manner as they create works that use scientific understanding in interesting and unusual ways.

Visual Arts (cont.)

Visual Observation

Observation is a critical skill for both artists and scientists as a tool for meaning making and understanding. Artists move beyond "ordinary looking" to uncover things that "otherwise might not be seen" (Harmon 2018).

Observation can be used to collect and record data, notice patterns, and capture cycles of change. This builds curiosity, generates interest, and can enable students to construct and test hypotheses and theories as well as experience real-world design elements such as line, shape, form, texture, pattern, and color.

Observation also creates opportunities for interpretation and meaning making. "Art and science both render ideas about the world into a form that allows the viewer to connect to the idea" (Zhu and Goyal 2019). Increasingly the arts are valued as an opportunity to build skills to notice, attend to, and perceive. Elliott Eisner notes: "We are given permission to slow down perception, to look hard, to savor the qualities that we try, under normal conditions, to treat so efficiently that we hardly notice they are there" (2002, 5).

Representation

David McCandless (2010) notes that we are overwhelmed by information and what he calls "data glut." He suggests that we work with representing information in new ways that prompt us to use our eyes. In this strategy, students create visual work, such as visual essays or infographics, to depict information. Translating scientific facts into visual form through this strategy can help students learn about science in fresh and meaningful ways. For example, students can explore the impact of disposable objects on home and school environments by collecting these objects and transforming them into visual artwork. When students represent scientific concepts through visual art, they translate their understanding into new forms, taking ownership of ideas, adding layers of meaning, and engaging with symbolism and metaphor.

Mixed Media

This strategy encourages students to experiment with putting a range of materials together in new ways. Students manipulate materials, experiment with the juxtaposition of materials, and create two- or three-dimensional pieces such as mobiles, collages, assemblages, dioramas, and digital installations. This process gives students the opportunity to use metaphors, prompting them to make meaning of experiences in new ways and boil concepts down to their essence to consider qualities rather than literal representations. Students test and explore ideas in experiential, hands-on ways; make choices about how they will use materials to communicate; and explore cause-and-effect relationships in the process of working with different media. The use of multiple representations is essential to the development of flexible thinking in science. This interpretive exploration will draw other themes. The construction of three-dimensional pieces requires students to interpret and explore ideas visually.

> "The importance of images and visual media in contemporary culture is changing what it means to be literate in the 21st century. Today's society is highly visual, and visual imagery is no longer supplemental to other forms of information."
>
> —Association of College and Research Libraries (2011, para. 1)

Visual Narrative

Model Lesson: Zines ROCK!

Overview

In this lesson, students work with teachers to create visual narratives called zines. Zines (short for "magazine" and pronounced ZEEN) are small, handcrafted reproducible booklets. Students find rocks in their own neighborhoods, classify them, observe them, draw them, and represent them in a variety of ways. In groups, students create a visual narrative and story about their rocks, which will form their science zines.

Materials

▸ magnifying glasses

▸ soft drawing instruments (pens, pencils, crayons, charcoal)

▸ paper for rubbing

▸ small sketchpads

▸ digital photo cameras with macro or close-up ability (*optional*)

▸ *Zine Template* (page 174)

▸ paper, scissors, glue sticks

▸ *How to Assemble a Zine* (pages 175–176)

▸ *Elements of Visual Art* (page 167)

Standards

Grades K–2

▸ Develops a model to represent the shapes and kinds of rocks on Earth

▸ Explores uses of materials and tools to create works of art or design

▸ Describes what an image represents

Grades 3–5

▸ Finds evidence of the effects of weathering or the rate of erosion by water, ice, wind, or vegetation in the formation of rocks

▸ Creates personally satisfying artwork using a variety of artistic processes and materials

▸ Determines messages communicated by an image

Grades 6–8

▸ Explains how rocks contain evidence of the minerals, temperatures, and forces that created them

▸ Demonstrates openness in trying new ideas, materials, methods, and approaches in making works of art

▸ Analyzes multiple ways that images influence specific audiences

Grades 9–12

▸ Investigates the properties of the hydrologic cycle and system interactions commonly known as the rock cycle

▸ Understands how the characteristics and structures of art are used to accomplish commercial, personal, communal, or other artistic intentions

Visual Narrative *(cont.)*

Preparation

Look up the word *zine* on the internet. Survey different definitions to familiarize yourself with the culture of zines, and select some age-appropriate models to show students. The Small Science Collective (**www.smallsciencecollective.org**) has multiple zines on science topics available as PDFs. You can find other zine templates by searching "zine template" on the internet.

Each group of students will need a collection of rocks that includes a variety of surface textures or type (sedimentary, metamorphic, and igneous rocks). Students can work with a rock collection they bring in from home, or you can have them find rocks outside. Additional suggestions are provided in the Specific Grade-Level Ideas.

Procedure

1. Ask students to bring in a few rocks from their neighborhood. Tell them to place each rock in a plastic bag with an index card that identifies where they found the rock.

2. Divide the class into groups of two or three. Work with students to identify classification categories that might include size, color, or texture. Have students in each group combine their rock collections and classify the rocks they brought according to the predetermined categories. Have each group present their rock findings to the class. Invite students to discuss the criteria used.

> "A zine is a self-published, non-commercial print-work that is usually produced in small quantities. Zines are created and bound in many DIY ways, but usually by making an original 'master flat,' and then photocopying, folding, and stapling the pages into simple pamphlets."
>
> —The Bindery (n.d., para. 4)

3. Introduce the concept of a zine. Share zine examples with the class. Ask students to identify characteristics of zines across examples. Invite students to discuss, in their opinion, what makes a zine successful. Encourage students to notice the way text and images link together, the way the space is used creatively, and the use of strong contrast (dark and light) to catch the viewer's eye. If students have made zines in the past, encourage them to bring in examples.

4. Tell students that each group will be a zine production team, which will produce a zine that tells a story about the rock cycle.

5. Distribute a magnifying glass, a soft pencil, paper for rubbings, a small sketchpad, and illustration pens to each zine production team.

6. Introduce the French term *frottage*, which is used by artists to describe a texture rubbing. Demonstrate for students how to create a rubbing by laying the paper over the rock and using a soft visual material such as pencil, chalk pastel, charcoal, or crayon. Instruct each team to make frottage rubbings of their rocks and use the magnifying glass to look at the rocks close up and then draw them. Also, have them draw the rock outline from different angles using an illustration pen. If available, have students use the macro feature on a digital camera to take highly detailed close-ups of the rocks.

7. Review the processes of the rock cycle, including the role of weathering, erosion, heat, and pressure, depending on your grade level standards.

Visual Narrative *(cont.)*

8. Instruct groups to create a short visual narrative that tells the story of their rocks. This story should include what they have learned about the rocks, including how they might have been formed and how they got their shape or texture.

9. Distribute several *Zine Template* activity sheets to each group, along with scissors, glue sticks, and illustration pens. Have students assemble their zines from the various visual elements and images they have produced. Students also can use text to supplement the information about their rocks.

10. Photocopy the zines, making enough for each student in class. Return the photocopied zines to their respective teams for students to fold. Distribute the *How to Assemble a Zine* activity sheet and have each group fold their zines.

11. Have students distribute their zines to the class. If desired, you can assess students' work and submit them to the Small Science Collective for publication (**www.smallsciencezines.blogspot.com**), provide a copy of the zines to the school library, or have students share their zines with other classes to teach them about rocks.

12. Use the Discussion Questions to debrief the activity.

Discussion Questions

▸ What does the texture of the rock tell us, and why was it important to show that in our artworks?

▸ How did you think about the sequencing of the pages of your zine?

▸ Which art technique (drawing, frottage, or photography) did you prefer, and why?

▸ Did the order of the pages matter in your story about rocks, why?

▸ What forces do you think acted on the rocks in your story to give them their shape and texture? How did you represent this visually in your zine?

▸ What did you learn about the processes of the rock cycle? How did you depict your understanding through your zine?

▸ What did you learn from drawing the rocks, exploring texture rubbings, and creating images of them?

▸ What did you learn from putting your zines together? What would you do differently?

Visual Narrative *(cont.)*

Specific Grade-Level Ideas

Grades K–2

Talk with students about the differences between rocks, pebbles, and sand. Have students work independently rather than in teams. Have each student create a single image of a rock and give it a name. Give students art supplies, such as colored pencils, crayons, paints, sand, and glue, to enhance their rock pictures. Collect the images and combine them into a class zine to create a visual narrative.

Grades 3–5

Students can work individually to create a zine that focuses on depicting one of the mechanical weathering processes, such as frost wedging, abrasion, or tree root wedging. Erosion processes also can be explored, such the effect erosion has on rocks from blowing wind, flowing water, and moving ice.

This strategy can be used to explore any scientific process, such as the change of seasons, natural cycles, and so on.

Grades 6–8

Have students go into detail about the different types of rocks and learn about and find evidence of various processes that affect rocks, such as the minerals, temperatures, and forces that created them.

Grades 9–12

Provide students with more complex zine templates to develop sophisticated stories that may not necessarily be linear.

Name: _____ Date: _____

Zine Template

Directions: Use this template to design your zine. The numbers (1 to 8) indicate the order of the pages for your zine. Fold a sheet of blank paper along the dotted lines shown on this template. Then, write and/or illustrate your narrative in the boxes. Remember to write or illustrate in the direction of the number in each box on the template.

2	1 (front)
3	8 (back)
4	7
5	6

(Numbers 1, 8, 7, 6 appear inverted/upside-down in the right column)

Name: _____ Date: _____

How to Assemble a Zine

Directions: Follow the steps to fold your story into a zine.

1. Design your zine, using the *Zine Template*.

2. Hold your zine design portrait and then fold in in half lengthwise. Use scissors to cut the zine as shown. Be careful not to cut beyond the indicated area.

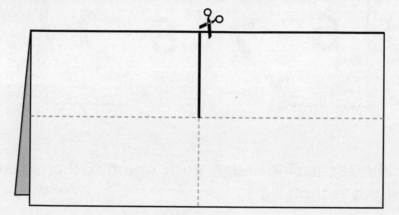

3. Unfold the zine design again. There should be a cut in the center.

Name: _____ Date: _____

How to Assemble a Zine (cont.)

4. Then, fold your zine design landscape so all the pages are on the outside as shown.

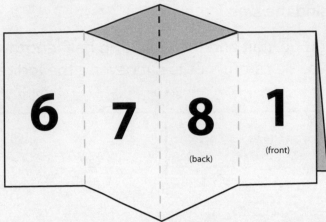

5. Pinching both sides of the zine design, push inward so that a diamond shape is created from the cut section.

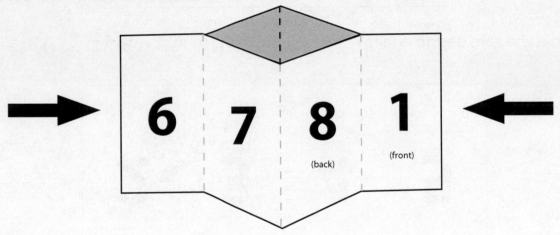

6. Fold the zine design so the pages go in the order of your narrative.

7. Your zine is complete!

Visual Experimentation

Model Lesson: Light Investigations

Overview

Experimentation is used extensively in both science and visual art. In this lesson, students experiment with light and shadow using a range of materials. After this period of experimentation, students apply their knowledge as they transform lamps, flashlights, mirrors, and other objects into light sculptures.

Materials

▸ white sheet, paper, or bare white wall for screen

▸ flashlights, hand-held mirrors

▸ sketchbooks and pencils

▸ *Light Experiment Documentation* (page 182)

▸ transparent objects such as color film sheets, plastic, water, bubbles *(optional)*

▸ examples of shadow art

▸ construction supplies such as wire, fishing line, construction paper, clay, tape

▸ *Elements of Visual Art* (page 167)

▸ camera to take pictures or video of students' art *(optional)*

Standards

Grades K–2

▸ Investigates how light travels in a straight line until it strikes an object

▸ Understands that learning happens when you make observations and conduct simple experiments

▸ Explores uses of materials and tools to create works of art or design

Grades 3–5

▸ Develops a model to explain that light can be reflected, absorbed, or refracted

▸ Creates an artist statement using art vocabulary to describe personal choices in art making

▸ Creates personally satisfying artwork using a variety of artistic processes and materials

Grades 6–8

▸ Develops a model to describe that light reflecting from objects can be scattered

▸ Develops a model to describe that light is absorbed or transmitted through materials

▸ Demonstrates openness in trying new ideas, materials, and approaches in making works of art

Grades 9–12

▸ Develops a model to describe that light is absorbed or transmitted through various materials

▸ Demonstrates acquisition of skills and knowledge in a chosen art form through experimentation and persistence

Visual Experimentation *(cont.)*

Preparation

Conduct an internet search for images of "shadow art" and select examples to share with students. Pieces of shadow art by artists Christian Boltanski and Kumi Yamashita are good examples. Select a bare wall in your classroom or hang a white sheet or large roll of paper on a wall to create a white backdrop. Be sure it is large enough for all students to work with, or you can create multiple backdrops to make the space larger. Experiment with making your own shadow piece in your classroom to ensure that all the variables will work (the level of darkness in the room, the distances, the space, and so on).

Review the physics of light so you can help explain to students what is happening as they experiment with light. Additional suggestions are provided in the Specific Grade-Level Ideas.

Procedure

1. Divide the class into groups of three and distribute flashlights, sketchbooks, and the *Light Experiment Documentation* activity sheet. Make sure the room is dim enough to track the light of a flashlight. Have one student in each group point light from a flashlight toward the white screen. Have a second student track the trajectory of the light by drawing an invisible line with their finger, or, to make this more concrete, have students use yarn to make the trajectory visible. Have the third student sketch what is happening on the *Light Experiment Documentation* activity sheet. Explain how light waves are traveling from point A (the flashlight) to point B (the screen).

2. Distribute hand-held mirrors and direct students to deflect the light and make it go in a different direction. Have them experiment with different angles. Tell students to track the angle of the light and document what they see on the *Light Experiment Documentation* activity

sheet. Discuss what is happening with the light waves and ask students to predict what would happen if they placed certain materials in the light trajectory.

3. Have students experiment with placing different materials in the light trajectory. Depending on age and accessibility, provide transparent plastic, water, bubbles, crystals, clear film of various colors, and objects that may be solid or transparent. Have students experiment with holding the objects and the light at different angles and from different distances. Tell students to document at least two additional experiments on their *Light Experiment Documentation* activity sheet.

4. Instruct students to experiment further and document what they see by considering shape, size, color, and the light source in their sketchbooks. Have students use lines to record the trajectory of the light toward the screen and to represent where they see light traveling to as well as the shapes the light makes on the screen or floor (if lit from above).

5. Share your selected examples of shadow art. Ask students what they see and what they notice. Ask questions such as "What kinds of images do the light and shadow make? What do those images make you think of? Do they remind you of anything in your own life? How do you think you might feel if you were alone in the room with the shadows?"

6. Tell students that they will now make their own artwork by using light and shadow. Make construction materials available, such as wire, fishing line, construction paper, clay, and tape. Tell students they are free to create their shadow art using any of the available materials.

Visual Experimentation (cont.)

7. Have students turn on their flashlights and darken the room. Allow time for students to experiment with objects and ideas. If students have trouble getting started, suggest they cut shapes from construction paper and experiment with ways of holding them in the light. They will need to find a way to anchor shapes, such as attaching them to wires stuck in clay or by hanging them with fishing line. Use the Planning Questions to help students develop their work.

8. Provide a set amount of time for students to edit and develop their pieces. Have them create sketches of their finished pieces in their sketchbooks.

9. Hold a class gallery walk around the room, lighting only one piece at a time. Have students sketch each piece in their sketchbooks, noting the trajectory of light in each. Use the Discussion Questions to debrief.

10. Because these works are temporary, document students' shadow art by photographing or videotaping each piece, if possible.

"Art and science are intrinsically linked; the essence of art and science is discovery. Both artists and scientists work in a systematic but creative way—knowledge and understanding are built up through pieces of art or a series of labs. In the classroom, integrating science and visual art can provide students with the latitude to think, discover, and make connections."

—Rebecca Alberts (2008, para. 1)

Planning Questions

‣ What is your artwork about?

‣ What emotion or idea do you want your piece to convey (mystery, quiet, reflection, fun, sadness)?

‣ How might you create shadows with sharp edges?

‣ How might you create shadows with soft edges?

‣ Do you want your artwork to be interactive? Do you want it to move?

‣ How will you use distance of objects in light to communicate ideas?

‣ How can you use your learning through experimentation (distance of objects, light angles, light sources, object opacity) to achieve your desired effect?

Discussion Questions

‣ What is your shadow work about and how did you decide on that topic?

‣ What did you notice about shadows as an artist? As a scientist?

‣ How can light and shadow affect the atmosphere in a room?

‣ What did you learn about how light behaves by creating your shadow art?

‣ How might you make a shadow art if you were working only with natural light?

‣ How and why did you change your work after your experimentation with light?

Visual Experimentation (cont.)

Specific Grade-Level Ideas

Grades K–2

Discuss light, shadow, and reflection with students, and then allow them to experiment with using their bodies to make shadows. If using a projector, students can get close to and far from the projector to see how their shadows get bigger and smaller.

Students can make shadow puppets by cutting out paper shapes and mounting them on craft sticks. Instead of focusing on the angles of light, students can draw what they see. Have students work either in small groups (each group can create puppets of animals that live in various habitats) or as a whole class to create a single piece.

Students also can experiment with making floating sculptures out of natural materials, paper, or plastic building blocks tied to string and investigate how the objects move by pulling, pushing, blowing, and more.

Have students document the process by taking two photographs of their artwork: one of the piece before light is applied and one in shadow after light is applied. Have students compare and contrast the images.

Grades 3–5

Have students make diagrams that show the angles at which light is refracted and to consider various ways in which light scatters.

You can integrate engineering and other forces of physics by asking students to develop freestanding pieces and/or hanging pieces that move, creating shifting shadows. Extend these ideas to the solar system and how light interacts at that level with the sun, the moon, and satellites.

Students can experiment to develop a sculpture that applies their knowledge of other science content, such as water (looking at currents, flotation, sinking, balance in relation to weight, density, and so on). For floating sculptures that take into account currents, look at Andy Goldsworthy's film *Rivers and Tides* and his other works in nature. After viewing Goldsworthy's work, students can investigate environmental issues as they do ephemeral sculptures, experimenting with natural materials outdoors.

You can use this strategy to explore engineering by having students experiment with materials to create machines. They can also integrate sound and movement to investigate additional content.

Visual Experimentation (cont.)

Specific Grade-Level Ideas (cont.)

Grades 6–8

Bring in more sophisticated notions of physics in terms of light by adding color as a variable and investigating light wave absorption, reflection, and scattering. This lesson provides a good foundation for learning about waves by having students work with an element that is visible. Extend this learning to sound waves and other kinds of waves.

Challenge students both in visual arts and engineering by having them make an interactive work that integrates visual imagery by using projected images to communicate something specific about a particular topic, such as weather, the solar system, or heat and energy. Have students integrate emotion by creating a piece that transforms when viewers interact with it, making the viewer reflect on a particular environmental issue. Students can push the idea of mood if they wish to convey a sense of urgency or of hope, for example.

Grades 9–12

View artwork by the artist duo Sue Webster and Tim Noble, who primarily use discarded food packaging as sculpture media to make a statement about the impact of humans' carbon footprint. Challenge students to build a sculpture from discarded materials that will communicate a message about the environmental impact of human activities, but only when light is shined through at a certain angle. Before starting, research the effect of disposable packaging on the planet. Invite students to consider how scientists can address this issue by developing technologies that produce less waste, and how artists can create a call to action through their work. Afterward, have students present their artworks and how they connect to their research findings, while highlighting their artistic choices.

Name: _____ Date: _____

Light Experiment Documentation

Directions: In each square, draw what you see. Include the light source, and follow its trajectory. Use lines to illustrate where the light goes.

Flashlight to screen	Flashlight to _____ to screen
Flashlight to _____ to screen Add any additional turns the light might take.	Flashlight to _____ to screen Add any additional turns the light might take.

    © Shell Education

Visual Observation

Model Lesson: Artful Lens to Scientific Observation

Overview

Observation is used in scientific processes to create detailed records of objects or events as evidence and as visual art to document and represent objects, relationships, and ideas. In this lesson, students closely observe a natural object. They study the object closely, record and document what they see as they draw it, and enlarge it using a grid. Students then put their enlarged drawings together to create a large-scale collaborative piece that includes all students' work.

Materials

▸ natural materials small enough to hold in the hand, such as moss, bark, rocks, leaves, shells, pinecones, grasses, feathers, and insects

▸ *Viewfinder Frame* (page 187)

▸ *Observation Drawing Template* (page 188)

▸ scissors

▸ *Magnification Grid* (page 189)

▸ art supplies, such as colored pencils, markers, pastels, paints, etc.

▸ *Elements of Visual Art* (page 167)

Standards

Grades K–2

▸ Develops a model to record patterns in the natural world

▸ Uses observation and investigation to prepare for making a work of art

▸ Interprets art by identifying subject matter and describing relevant details

Grades 3–5

▸ Analyzes and interprets data to provide evidence about what happens in the world

▸ Identifies and demonstrates diverse methods of artistic investigation

▸ Interprets art by analyzing characteristics of form and structure and visual elements

Grades 6–8

▸ Understands that science knowledge is based on observations and conceptual connections between evidence and explanations

▸ Designs a method to gather, analyze, and interpret scientific data

▸ Develops criteria to guide making a work of art that meets an identified goal

▸ Interprets art by analyzing subject matter and characteristics of form and structure

Grades 9–12

▸ Develops a model to show results of scientific investigations, experiments, and observations

▸ Applies media, techniques, and processes with sufficient skill, confidence, and sensitivity that one's intentions are carried out in artworks

Visual Observation (cont.)

Preparation

Search the internet for artwork that features detailed observation drawings from nature and select examples to share with students (such as works by Georgia O'Keefe, Ellsworth Kelly, Cathy Riley, Margaret Mee, and Clair Walker Leslie). Using the directions in the Procedure, create an example of a gridded image to show students. Collect natural materials, such as leaves, rocks, flowers, or pinecones for students to work from, or make plans to go outside as a class to collect materials prior to beginning the lesson. Additional suggestions are provided in the Specific Grade-Level Ideas.

Procedure

1. Ask students to select a natural object to work with. Invite them to spend a few quiet moments observing the object. Discuss the details students observe. Ask students to brainstorm places where they see patterns, shapes, textures, and so on in the objects.

2. Distribute the *Viewfinder Frame* and the Observation Drawing Template activity sheets and tell students they will be doing an observational drawing. Point out that the square on the *Observation Drawing Template* activity sheet is the same size as the square on the *Viewfinder Frame* activity sheet.

3. Have students cut out the square on the *Viewfinder Frame* activity sheet and use the hole as a window to look at and frame the object or a portion of the object. Then have students reproduce the image they see on the *Observation Drawing Template* activity sheet. Ask them to be intentional about using elements of art while sketching to observe.

4. Show artistic examples or demonstrate how to use the viewfinder to sketch for observation versus relying on imagination to embellish. Invite students to notice how the viewfinder allows them to focus on the details of the subject and eliminates background distractions. Tell them to capture the object as accurately as possible on the *Observation Drawing Template* activity sheet.

5. Ask students to look at their drawings. Ask: "Is your drawing fairly accurate? How is the drawing different from what you see? Is there anything you can add to make your drawing more accurate?" Invite students to refine their pieces by comparing the original object in nature with their drawings.

6. Tell students that they will now magnify their image by using a grid. In doing so, students can observe how scale has the ability to transform an object in a way that allows for creative design possibilities. Distribute the *Magnification Grid* activity sheet and tell students to draw each section of the object from the *Observation Drawing Template* in an equivalent square on the *Magnification Grid*. Have students notice the relationship between line and shape within the square and replicate it in the larger square. Encourage them to continue to refer to the original object throughout the process. When they are finished, they will have a magnified version of their original object.

7. Ask students to check their drawings for accuracy and revise as necessary. Once their magnified drawings are complete, photocopy them and set them aside.

8. Distribute art supplies and invite students to transform the object on their *Magnification Grid* activity sheet through different artistic techniques. They can add color, make lines darker or lighter, increase the contrast, and so on. Tell students that they should transform their drawing to

Visual Observation (cont.)

create an aesthetically interesting image imbued with a sense of interest. Share the selected examples of art to inspire students.

9. Have students work together to create a display of all their artworks on a classroom bulletin board or wall. Consider displaying all versions of their artworks in progress (initial sketch using the viewfinder, magnified drawing, and enhanced drawing with inclusion of artistic techniques). By doing this, students can see the drawing of the object created with the accurate black-and-white drawings against the artwork created with their transformed pieces. Use the Discussion Questions to debrief.

Discussion Questions

▸ How did the *Viewfinder Frame* help you see your object differently?

▸ How did the observation drawing allow you to focus closely?

▸ How does scale or magnification play a role in your observation?

▸ How did transforming the drawing into a new art piece make it different from the original image?

▸ Which artistic choices did you make in transforming your final image?

▸ How are the two grids different (the grid displaying photocopied work and the grid displaying the transformed work)?

▸ Why might a scientist spend time closely observing an object in nature?

▸ How might drawing allow you to collect, analyze, and interpret data?

Visual Observation (cont.)

Specific Grade-Level Ideas

Grades K–2

If possible, take students outside to look for patterns in nature. Students can gather leaves and look at tree trunks and other natural elements. Have students use the *Viewfinder Frame* activity sheet to find and view a pattern in nature. If students find patterns that have texture, such as rocks, they can do crayon rubbings instead of line drawings. Students also can glue natural objects (leaves, twigs, flowers) to sheets of paper to represent their patterns.

Grades 6–8

Have students use a microscope to significantly magnify small natural elements (for example, insects and leaves) and draw the visual details they see.

Have students work with similar objects across different scientific families. For example, they can explore different kinds of seed cones from conifers. Challenge students to compare and contrast their drawings to notice subtle differences between objects.

Grades 3–5

Have students use a magnifying glass to search for details that are not easily noticed by the naked eye. Ask them to select an object, view it under the magnifying glass, and frame it with their *Viewfinder Frame*. Have students draw the magnified image on the *Observation Drawing Template* before enlarging it with the *Magnification Grid*. Ask students to think about how they could bring out some of the elements that they see by emphasizing a particular element with color or by making elements darker and more prominent.

Students can use this strategy to observe, record, and transform any visual element of scientific study such as landscape patterns, skin texture (pores and hairs), and so on.

Grades 9–12

Have students explore how scientists observe nature to create innovative technology. For example, review *Biomimicry: Innovation Inspired by Nature* by Janine M. Benyus. Have students find patterns in nature and experiment with the scale of the patterns to transfer ideas into the design and engineering of functional objects.

Name: _____ Date: _____

Viewfinder Frame

Directions: Cut out the square and use this sheet of paper as a window to look at patterns in nature.

Name: _____ Date: _____

Observation Drawing Template

Directions: Draw what you see in the *Viewfinder Frame*. Draw the pattern as accurately as you see it in your *Viewfinder Frame,* noticing where each form and line is in the frame.

Name: _____ Date: _____

Magnification Grid

Directions: Look at your drawing on the *Observation Drawing Template*, and transfer the marks in each small square into the equivalent large square on this grid. Try to make it as accurate as possible.

Representation

Model Lesson: Exploring Environmental Impact

Overview

In this lesson, students collect, analyze, classify, and organize disposable objects to investigate their function and impact in home and school environments. Students collect the disposable items their families and schools use over the course of one week and transform them into visual artwork that elicits an emotional response by representing the impact of disposable objects on our environment.

Materials

- examples of trash art and found object art
- *Object Classification* (pages 195–196)
- large sheets of cardboard or poster board
- tape, glue, or staplers
- measuring tapes
- disposable objects (paper towel rolls, jars, egg cartons, cardboard boxes, and so on)
- *Impact Data Questionnaire* (page 197)
- *Elements of Visual Art* (page 167)

Standards

Grades K–2

- Develops a simple sketch or physical model to illustrate how to solve a given problem
- Communicates solutions that will reduce the impact of humans on the land, water, air, and/or other living things
- Describes what an image represents
- Uses observation and investigation in preparation for making a work of art

Grades 3–5

- Investigates how engineers improve technologies or develop new ones to increase their benefits and decrease known risks
- Determines messages communicated by an image
- Identifies and demonstrates diverse methods of artistic investigation

Grades 6–8

- Constructs an argument supported by evidence for how increases in human population and consumption of natural resources impact Earth's systems
- Analyzes multiple ways that images influence specific audiences
- Develops criteria to guide making a work of art that meets an identified goal

Grades 9–12

- Evaluates a technological solution that reduces the impact of human activities on natural systems
- Understands how the characteristics and structures of art are used to accomplish commercial, personal, communal, or other artistic intentions

Representation (cont.)

Preparation

Conduct an internet search for images of artists who work with recycled materials and select examples of found object art to share with students. Examples include the Guerra de la Paz collective, Chiharu Shiota, Tadashi Kawamata, Lee Boroson, and Paul Matosic. If desired, search for and select images and videos about the Great Pacific Garbage Patch to show students.

Consider the space you want to use for the installation. This could be inside the classroom, including the floor and/or walls, or, with appropriate permission, this could extend beyond your classroom into school hallways.

Ask students to collect disposable objects at home for one week, such as toilet or paper towel rolls, small cardboard boxes, egg cartons, or jars. You also can ask students to gather all the disposable things they use in school throughout the week. All objects should be clean and dry before beginning the activity. Additional suggestions are provided in the Specific Grade-Level Ideas.

Procedure

1. Share with students the definition of *disposable*. Then ask students to look around the classroom and think about their daily routines. Ask, "What disposable materials do you use?"

2. Ask students: "Why do you think anyone would design disposable objects? Are there objects we would want to use only once? Why? What are the benefits of disposable objects? What unintended impact might disposable objects have on the environment?"

3. Next ask students, "Where do you think objects go once they are used and thrown out?" Discuss where many of the objects end up—in landfills or the ocean. If desired, share images, facts, or videos about the Great Pacific Garbage Patch. Share alternative solutions and conservation practices, including reducing consumption or reusing or recycling products as well as using engineered alternatives such as biodegradable plastics made from plants.

4. Introduce the definition of an *artistic installation* as a "three-dimensional visual artwork, often created for a specific place . . . and designed to change the perception of space" (Fox 2017).

5. Explain to students that they will create an art installation that represents the disposable objects they collected. Share examples of the work of artists who use found objects. Ask students to identify what they notice about the works and what is visually impactful about them. "What elements do the artists use to organize the materials? Do you see any patterns? What is emotionally impactful about the artworks? What are they about?"

6. Distribute the *Object Classification* activity sheet. Have students gather the disposable objects they brought in, classify 10 of those items, note them in the chart, and answer the questions. This will help them select classification criteria for their artworks.

7. Divide the class into groups of four and provide each group with space to experiment with various ways of laying out their disposable objects. Have them group their objects, spread them out, and organize them based on one or two criteria described in the chart. Ask them to consider how certain patterns and colors may create emotion. Have them create their pieces by laying the objects on a large sheet of cardboard or poster board. Introduce the notion of *composition* in art as the "arrangement of elements within a work of art" (Tate, n.d., para. 1). Objects can remain

Representation (cont.)

loose or be glued, taped, or stapled onto the cardboard or poster board.

8. Show students the designated space for their art installation of disposable objects. Ask students to consider how the space might be transformed by the installation. Challenge groups to organize their pieces into a larger class piece. They can put their arranged pieces side-by-side, in a long line, or in a flowing shape to resemble a river or other formation.

9. Distribute measuring tape and the *Impact Data Questionnaire* activity sheet. Ask students to look at the class piece, measure it, and record their responses to the questionnaire. Discuss and compare results.

10. Use the Discussion Questions to debrief and develop a plaque that includes the title of the artwork, the size, the materials used, the date, a short explanation of the creative process, and the meaning of the work.

Discussion Questions

▸ What criteria did you use to organize your objects into a composition?

▸ What objects are in your artwork? What do they make you think of?

▸ Look at the whole installation. What do you notice? What does it make you think of?

▸ What did you learn about humans' effect on Earth from this process?

▸ What title would you give this art installation?

"Art-based activities can help students comprehend abstract scientific theories and improve their critical thinking skills. Through the manipulation of images and materials, these activities can also address deficits in sequencing and visual-spatial relationships. With each visual interpretation of a scientific concept, it is important that the student can show an understanding of the connection between the image/object and the concept."

—Rebecca Alberts (2008, para. 4)

Representation (cont.)

Specific Grade-Level Ideas

Grades K–2

Ask students to think about particular situations that they are familiar with, such as a birthday party, and have them consider the many things that get thrown away afterward (wrapping paper, balloons, plastic goody bags, and more). Have students focus on the functions of discarded objects and transform them into festive party supplies (for example, making garlands with remnants of ribbons and wrapping paper cut into small shapes). Culminate with a class celebration that focuses on sustainable practices. Ask students to suggest what else they can do to minimize waste, such as using reusable cups and dishes or making decorations, tablecloths, or wrapping paper out of used paper or plastic.

Grades 3–5

Have students focus on the benefits of technology and its costs to the environment. They can compare reusable containers with disposable containers, and track their life cycle to compare costs and benefits of both types of containers. Students also can use this strategy to consider the volume of other manufactured goods, such as plastic toys. The work of artist Tara Donovan, who makes art out of large amounts of objects such as buttons, tape, pencils, and polystyrene cups, is a good resource. Challenge students to take into account things we keep that we do not need.

This strategy also can be used to investigate the nature of scientific inquiry as it supports observation, classification, and data analysis. Students can use this strategy to represent unity and diversity within any population such as animals, insects, plants, or food. Or it can be used to represent weather by asking students to represent how much rain or snow falls in various areas using images of water drops or snowflakes.

Representation (cont.)

Specific Grade-Level Ideas (cont.)

Grades 6–8

As an extension, have students investigate the effects of disposable objects in other places. For example, they can investigate natural habitats uninhabited by humans that end up full of our disposable garbage. They can investigate the North Atlantic Garbage Patch and develop work that focuses on the impact of our trash on the ocean and the coasts. With this focus, they also can learn about ocean currents and how they interact with human technology for better and for worse. *Tracking Trash: Flotsam, Jetsam, and the Science of Ocean Motion* by Loree Griffin Burns is a great book for this level. The strategy also can be extended to address human population and its impact on any ecosystem.

Grades 9–12

In addition to the suggestions for grades 6–8, have students identify the five major ocean gyres (the North Atlantic Gyre, the South Atlantic Gyre, the South Pacific Gyre, the North Pacific Gyre, and the Indian Ocean Gyre) and any respective garbage patches that result from ocean currents in those areas. Students can create visual representations that express the feelings and emotions of negatively impacted wildlife or ecosystems. After students identify the five major ocean gyres, have them conduct research to discover the different types of pollutants in each ocean gyre, comparing the gyre, the pollutants, and the surrounding human populations that contribute to the formation of these oceanic garbage patches.

Name: _____ Date: _____

Object Classification

Directions: Choose 10 disposable objects and describe them in this chart. Experiment with organizing your objects according to one or two criteria. Then answer the questions to help you determine the final organization of your objects.

Color										
Size										
Shape										
Reusable, Biodegradable, or Recyclable										
Material										
Function										
Object										

Representation

Object Classification (cont.)

1. Which objects have the greatest visual impact?

   _____

   _____

   _____

   _____

2. Which have the greatest emotional impact?

   _____

   _____

   _____

   _____

3. Which objects will you use in your final installation? Why?

   _____

   _____

   _____

   _____

   _____

4. What criteria will you use to organize the objects? Why?

   _____

   _____

   _____

   _____

   _____

   © Shell Education

Name: _____ Date: _____

Impact Data Questionnaire

Directions: Look at the final piece and answer the questions.

1. Measure the class installation. How much space does it take up?

> Our classroom installation measures _____ square feet.

2. How much space would an installation take up that includes disposable objects from all the classrooms in your school?

> (_____ number of classrooms in your school
>
> x _____ square feet of display per classroom)
>
> All the disposable objects in all the classrooms in our school would
>
> measure about _____ square feet.

3. How much space would an installation take up that includes the disposable objects from all schools in your city?

> (_____ number of schools in your city
>
> x _____ square feet of display per school)
>
> All the disposable objects in all the schools in our city would
>
> measure about _____ square feet.

Mixed Media

Model Lesson: Collage and the Changing Earth

Overview

In this lesson, students use mixed media to investigate and represent the earth and how it changes during geological processes. They use various materials to create diptychs that include before and after representations of a location and show the effect forces have on the earth, such as rain, deforestation, volcanic activity, global warming, and the movement of plate tectonics.

Materials

▸ *Planning Guide* (page 202)

▸ *Diptych Template* (page 203)

▸ heavyweight 11" × 14" paper

▸ scissors, glue, crayons, and/or colored pencils

▸ other kinds of paper such as tissue paper, scrap paper, magazines, and so on (optional)

▸ *Elements of Visual Art* (page 167)

Standards

Grades K–2

▸ Conducts an investigation to describe different materials on Earth

▸ Understands that a model can be used to learn about the real object

▸ Creates art that tells a story about a life experience

▸ Makes art with various materials and tools to explore personal interests and questions

Grades 3–5

▸ Uses several sources to provide evidence that Earth events can occur quickly or slowly

▸ Understands that models can be used to represent and predict changes in objects and processes

▸ Applies knowledge of resources and tools to investigate ideas through art making

▸ Identifies and analyzes cultural associations suggested by visual imagery

Grades 6–8

▸ Interprets data on landforms to provide evidence of past plate motions

▸ Knows models are used to think about things that cannot be investigated directly

▸ Formulates an artistic investigation of personally relevant content

▸ Analyzes ways that visual components and cultural associations influence ideas and emotions

Grades 9–12

▸ Evaluates evidence of the past and current movements of continental and oceanic crust and the theory of plate tectonics

▸ Applies media, techniques, and processes with sufficient skill, confidence, and sensitivity that one's intentions are carried out in artworks

Mixed Media (cont.)

Preparation

Consider the geological forces you want students to investigate and browse the internet for images of how Earth's surface is affected by those forces. You can focus on natural forces, such as wind, water, melting glaciers, or volcanoes, or you can focus on human forces to investigate deforestation, construction, and overgrazing. Select both aerial and ground images to share with students for reference.

Gather art materials and cut sheets of 11" × 14" heavy paper in half the long way so there are strips of paper that measure about 5.5" × 14". Students will fold each strip in half so they have two connected panels (like a two-page book).

Ideally, make your own diptych to share with students to foresee and resolve any potential glitches in the process. Additional suggestions are provided in the Specific Grade-Level Ideas.

> "Collages are a means for students to gather and assemble images that represent an idea. This is especially appealing for students who are self-conscious about their perceived lack of artistic abilities. When students are making collages in science, the collage grows out of completed research. Having background information allows the students to make critical choices when looking for appropriate images to represent written facts."
>
> —Rebecca Alberts (2008, para. 8)

Procedure

1. Introduce students to forces that change the earth. Ask them if they have ever noticed ways in which the ground changes, such as when running water makes a path in loose soil. Share other examples they may have seen, such as a bulldozer digging into the ground, and ask them if they can think of other ways in which the landscape changes.

2. Share images you gathered and discuss with students how various forces shape the landscape of the earth. Ask them to notice the marks on the landscape and consider how they were formed.

3. Tell students that they will be investigating a place affected by a particular force, and they will make diptychs to represent how the landscape has changed. Explain that a *diptych* is a work of art with two connected panels that form one complete piece. Tell students that one side of their diptychs will represent the landscape *before* change and the other side will represent the landscape *after* it has been transformed. Remind students that the earth changes constantly and they are to choose only two moments in time.

4. Distribute the *Planning Guide* activity sheet and allow students to choose the place they will represent in their diptychs. Have them look at past and present images of their location by conducting research about the area. Direct students to use the *Planning Guide* to help them develop ideas for their diptychs.

5. Distribute the *Diptych Template* activity sheet and have students roughly sketch their idea.

6. Tell students they will create their diptychs using the technique called *collage*. Define the word *collage* and share examples of collage artists, such as Romare Bearden, Hannah Hoch, Kurt Schwitters, and Deborah Lawrence. Demonstrate and explain that they will cut and/or tear apart materials and glue them to paper, overlapping pieces and creating texture to represent the earth. Ask students to use the principles of design to guide their process.

Mixed Media (cont.)

7. Tell students they will create texture and color for their collages by doing rubbings. This color and texture will represent the earth. Model this process by placing a sheet of white paper on a textured surface and coloring it with the side of a crayon or pencil to capture the texture. Tell students they also can paint, crumple, or tear paper such as magazine paper, newspaper, or tissue paper in addition to using found textures. Allow time for students to plan their collages, using information from the *Planning Guide* activity sheet.

8. Distribute the 5.5" × 14" strips of paper. Have students fold their strips in half to create two sides that open like the pages of a book. Provide scissors, glue, and time for students to cut, tear, and glue materials to create their diptychs. Tell students they also can layer the paper to create a sense of volume or relief if they want to represent a raised surface from an aerial perspective.

9. Have students exhibit their finished diptychs on their desks. Then have them take a gallery walk around the classroom to view the different artworks. Use the Discussion Questions to debrief and critique the work.

Drawn from the French term *coller* [ko-LÉ], meaning "to glue," *collage* is "an artistic composition made of various materials (such as paper, cloth, or wood) glued on a surface" (Merriam-Webster, n.d., para. 1).

Discussion Questions

▸ What shapes and textures do you see in the various collages?

▸ What materials were used to achieve the colors, shapes, and textures?

▸ What kinds of terrain and material do they represent?

▸ How are the two images in the diptych different from each other?

▸ How does having two images help you visualize the effects forces can have on the earth?

▸ How did the artist communicate before and after images using visual elements?

▸ Do any of the collages elicit an emotional response? How and why?

▸ How did each artist use elements of visual art and principles of design?

Mixed Media (cont.)

Specific Grade-Level Ideas

Grades K–2

Have students investigate what the earth is made of. Take students outside to look at the ground right beneath their feet. They can dig up and gather samples of the different things that make up the ground (soil, little rocks, some roots, and so on). Students can experiment with what happens when some of those elements interact with water (for example, pouring soil and rocks into a clear water container). They can then experiment with materials, including natural objects from the earth, to create a collage that represents what the earth is made of. Students also can use collage to represent various forms of life with natural materials such as plants.

Grades 3–5

Students can focus on the multiple ways in which the earth gradually changes. For example, they can construct collages that represent weathering, erosion, or sediment created by atmospheric forces such as wind or water. Students also can consider how each of these changes affects our experience on the planet. If possible, they can observe the phenomena at the beach and consider seashells. Or students can think about the weathering of soil, and observe how it affects not just humans but also animals.

Have students play around with scale. Have students work in small groups to create a large-scale diptych.

Grades 6–8

Students can investigate plate tectonics by developing a diptych based on a particular place. Students can work in groups to investigate the geological phenomena that affect the Hawaiian Islands, Iceland, and the Rocky Mountains. Students should use deductive reasoning to determine which type of plate movement is involved and which type of boundary is created. This strategy also can be used to develop models of other scientific concepts such as the lithosphere. Students also can focus on the life sciences by imagining the human impact on particular ecosystems. They can consider how human activity impacts particular populations of animals or organisms by imagining them in their habitats before and after particular events.

Grades 9–12

Students can go into depth about the causes (for example, heat and gravitational forces) and effects (for example, earthquakes and volcanic eruptions) of plate tectonics. Have students collect images that represent a particular area of the globe to research. Their models could include two sides, one side representing Earth's surface that shows details, such as the boundaries of each plate, and one side including arrows that indicate the direction of its movement.

Students also could address the specific short-term and long-term effects different forms of technology have on their local area. They can investigate the potential impact of technologies that support the health and conservation of Earth (such as those used to prevent erosion or conserve energy).

Name: _____ Date: _____

Planning Guide

Directions: Research the area you will represent and complete this chart. Use your research and the images you found to describe the location before and after the change.

Ecosystem or landscape: _____

	First Image: Before Change	**Second Image: After Change**
Description of the ecosystem or landscape		
Select a force that affects the landscape		
Natural elements (soil, rock, water, ice, and so on)		
Colors		
Textures		

Name: _____   Date: _____

Diptych Template

Directions: Sketch your collage. Then, use your sketch as a guide for selecting colored and textured paper to use in your diptych.

After

Before

Creative Movement

Understanding
Creative Movement

Strategies for
Creative Movement

Answer Me in
Movement

Movement Strings

Progressions

Sensory Movement

Choreographic
Structure

Creative Movement

Understanding Creative Movement

Integrating creative movement across the curriculum is an engaging approach to learning that allows students to experience, translate, and communicate scientific ideas kinesthetically. In 1983, Howard Gardner identified bodily kinesthetic intelligence within his theory of multiple intelligences (2011) as one way that students learn. Neuroscientists are finding that memory and recall are improved when the body is engaged in the learning process (Zull 2002) and that the mind uses the body to make sense of ideas (Carpenter 2011).

While important for all learners, opportunities to express themselves nonverbally can be particularly powerful for some students, especially those for whom the current educational systems do not respond to their learning styles. Such opportunities can provide students with access to science content that would not be possible otherwise. Stacey Skoning (2008) states that creative movement, or dance, "is important to incorporate into our inclusive classrooms if we want to meet the needs of more diverse groups of students" (9).

Creative movement allows students to be physically active, which often increases students' attention span, but it is much more than just the incorporation of movement into classroom activities. When students are involved in creative movement, they become more mindful of their bodies' ability to communicate, explore what happens when they move with intention, engage in problem solving through movement, and develop awareness of their creative choices. It is important to keep the possibilities for this work in mind as students explore these lessons.

As students deconstruct and reconstruct concepts, they take ownership of the ideas through kinesthetic means and creative choices. Writer and choreographer Susan Griss (1994) makes the point that because creative movement is "expressive, informative, and analytical," it can heighten learning by increasing comprehension, providing multicultural insights, bolstering social skills, and focusing energy into creative outlets.

> Creative movement embraces an every body spirit. All the activities can be done seated or standing, stationary or ambulatory.
>
> —Celeste Miller, Choreographer and Educator (personal communication, May 4, 2021)

Elements of Creative Movement

These elements are drawn from several sources, including the Kennedy Center (Bodensteiner 2019), PBS Learning Media (KQED 2015), the Institute for Arts Integration and STEAM (Riley 2017), the National Core Arts Standards, and the Perpich Center for Arts Education (2009).

- **Body**: Creative movement works with the parts of the body to move, isolate, and manipulate to create shape and movement through space.
- **Space**: Creative movement interacts with and occupies space on different levels, in different pathways, in different size and scope of movement.
- **Action**: *Non-locomotor*, which is axial-movement around the body's axis and *locomotor*, movement that travels through space
- **Time**: Movement happens over time and can communicate through tempo and rhythm.
- **Energy**: The qualities (sustained, percussive, suspended, etc.), weight (heavy, light, etc.), and flow (continuous, controlled, etc.) of how movement occurs

Creative Movement (cont.)

Strategies for Creative Movement

Each creative movement strategy results in a short piece of choreography: repeatable dances made up of original movements created by students. The final strategy, Choreographic Structure is an advanced step in this process that introduces students to several tools of choreography and the suite form.

Answer Me in Movement

Students respond to a question from the teacher, and, instead of answering with words, they "answer" by creating their own movement to express their response. This could be as simple as an arm gesture such as circling the arms over the head to represent the sun. Answer Me in Movement invites students to develop the skill of translating ideas into new forms, exploring the meaning of concepts in new ways.

Movement Strings

Students invent a series of movements that can be strung together, similar to beads on a string. This strategy works well with lists of ideas that can be organized sequentially.

Progressions

Students focus on the transitions between their movements. It is a further development of Movement Strings. This strategy provides an opportunity to connect concepts, processes, and events into a movement phrase that links ideas together in meaningful ways.

Sensory Movement

Students use the five senses, combined with motion, as the inspiration to create movement. This strategy explores the sensory details of ideas. Perfect for figurative and connotative language, Sensory Movement invites students to experience the qualities of concepts such as colors, emotions, and more.

Choreographic Structure

In each creative movement strategy students are creating dances. This is choreography. Choreography begins with improvisation to create original movements and experiment with different ways to do them: fast or slow, big or little, and so on. From this experimentation the choreographer (or collaborative choreographers) selects the movements they want to use and orders them into sequences and patterns. This is called a *dance suite*. These now predetermined movements are repeatable. Students then rehearse the movements to prepare for their presentation. In this strategy, students are introduced to five choreographic structures to create a dance suite.

> "A dance suite can be thought of as a set of 'mini-dances' about the same topic or theme."
>
> —Celeste Miller,
> Choreographer and Educator (personal communication, May 4, 2021)

Creative Movement (cont.)

Choreography in the Classroom

Each of the creative movement strategies has been used successfully in classrooms by choreographer and educator Celeste Miller. The strategies are organized to build on each other, increasing in depth and complexity. Thus, it is highly recommended that you introduce the strategies to students in the order presented in this section:

1. Answer Me in Movement

2. Movement Strings

3. Progressions

4. Sensory Movement

5. Choreographic Structure

Students can move through the strategies sequentially, culminating in a short choreographed piece, or the strategies can be completed individually as one-time lessons.

All activities can be done in the classroom by moving tables/desks and seats to the outskirts of the room in an organized fashion. You also may take this process outside, use an open meeting area, or plan to use another open space such as the gym or cafeteria. A large space is not necessary for this process, but rather just another possibility. Students should stand in a circle formation with the teacher when given instructions and when sharing their creative products. Student breakout groups can be scattered throughout the room.

In the creative movement lesson plans, the word *dance* is used as a noun—"what is created"—and also as a verb—"to dance." We often think of dance as steps done to music, with a beat. In creative movement, dance encompasses unique motions created by the individual to express ideas. Creative movement dances can be done to silence or to words, in addition to music. Creative movement is unique and does not have

to mimic the steps or a particular dance genre (though it can). In the lesson plans, students are often referred to as "dancers." This is to empower students to own their agency as creative makers using dance. Teachers should make the decision to use the word based on the climate of their classroom; sometimes the word *dance* carries cultural or gendered overtones that inhibit student participation. Good substitute words for *dance* are *movement* (verb) or *movers* (noun). Teachers can refer to what their students are making as "creative movement explorations," instead of "dances." This is at your discretion.

Teaching the Strategies

Because these strategies build on each other, the first set of how-to lessons (pages 211–222) models how to introduce each strategy to students. The second set of lessons (pages 223–248) models one way to use the strategies with a single piece of text—*Living Sunlight: How Plants Bring the Earth to Life* by Molly Bang and Penny Chisholm. Each strategy allows the students to use movement to further investigate the text, its meaning, and its importance, culminating in a combination of all the movements (strategies) into one choreographed piece. Should you choose to use a different text with students, the lessons can serve as a guide to your thinking. Look for these characteristics in identifying texts that work well with movement:

▸ richly detailed visual and sensory images

▸ a sense of progression (the story moves along)

▸ language that evokes movement

▸ multigenre and multimodal texts—you can use an excerpt of a larger work (a letter, poem, monologue, visualization, primary source photograph, painting, quotation, or oral history)

Creative Movement (cont.)

Helpful Terms

- **Dance**: Movement aware of itself done with purpose. These movements may be unique to each person who creates them.

- **Movement**: Individual movements, often gestures. These are discrete units that can be organized in any order. Movements or gestures are the equivalent of a "word" in a sentence.

- **Movement sequence**: The stringing together of several discrete movements. Movement sequences can be thought of as "sentences."

- **Choreography**: Purposeful movements arranged for effect to communicate ideas.

- **Choreography tools**: Forms that can be used to create movement patterns.

- **Shape**: A frozen pose that you hold. A shape is not limited to circle, square, triangle, and so on. Rather it is the design of the body, similar to a sculpture, that can be held in stillness. Shapes are done with the whole body. For example: Stand on one foot, with the free leg bent and the toe touching the standing leg knee. Arms are straight out to the side.

- **Level**: Levels are where the body is on a vertical plane: low, middle, or high. You could be close to the ground (low), or as high as you can reach (high), or in between high and low (middle).

Music is a helpful tool to use with students in creative movement. Check out this creative movement Spotify playlist curated by choreographer and educator Celeste Miller: **open.spotify.com/playlist/7bvVFJ1Zj0 gJgC1wv1Bwsz**. You can use this playlist with any of the lessons in this section.

- **Neutral stance**: This is a resting stance, whether seated or standing. A student once defined a neutral stance this way: "It's like when a car is in neutral. It's not moving yet, but it is ready to go."

- **Call and response**: The leader does a movement, then the group responds by repeating the same movement back to the leader.

- **Copying**: The leader's back is to the group, and the group copies the leader. Thus the leader's right arm is the copier's right arm. If the leader moves to their right, everyone moves to their right.

- **Mirroring**: The leader faces the group. The group sees the leader as a mirror image. Thus the leader's right arm, is the group's left arm. If the leader moves to their right, the group moves to their left.

- **Unison**: Everyone is doing the same thing at the same time in sync with one another.

- **Counter unison**: Endless versions and configurations of how different people are doing different things.

- **Transition**: The ability to connect movement ideas (for example, a person can go from skipping to walking or from reaching upward to twisting around themselves).

- **Fan**: One person does a movement while everyone else is still, then the second person does a movement while everyone else is still, and so on. Every student gets a turn, then the movements are completed in reverse order.

- **Rondo**: Dancers perform their individual movements in unique sequences, so everyone in the group must learn everyone else's movement. Each dancer completes each movement but in a different order from the rest.

- **Recurrence**: The repetition of something that has been done in a dance before, but usually with a slight twist.

Introducing the Strategies

Answer Me in Movement Introduction

1. Explain to students that in the Answer Me in Movement strategy, we use our bodies instead of words to communicate an idea. We do this by creating a single-movement response based on a prompt. Tell students to think of the movement as a gesture, similar to the common gestures of using a wave to say "hello" or your pinky and thumb to say "call me."

One way to help students understand Answer Me in Movement is to reference the "live" function on a smartphone camera, where there is a slight bit of movement before the photo still is captured.

2. Share with students that you are going to give them a prompt, and you want them to show their movements en masse, which means "all together." Explain to students that they stay frozen at the end of their movement, thus creating a "snapshot" moment that nonverbally expresses their response to the prompt. Then, on your instruction to release, students should return to a neutral position. Say: "When I clap, I want you to answer me in movement, what is . . . ? When I clap again, go back to a neutral position."

   Example:

   Teacher: Answer me in movement, what is the weather today? *(Clap)*

   Students respond in movement with a unique original gesture that indicates today's weather; for example on a sunny day one student may make a circle with her arms to indicate the sun and another student may turn his face upward and smile to indicate sunshine falling welcomingly on his face.

After a short pause in which all students are frozen in their "answer," clap and have students relax into a neutral position.

3. Give each student a chance to show their movement and then share verbally what the movement represented and why it was their movement choice. **Note**: We never try to guess what a movement means; rather, this final step in the process gives students an opportunity to verbally share their movement-choice reasoning.

Introducing the Strategies *(cont.)*

Movement Strings Introduction

1. Explain to students that the Movement Strings strategy builds on the Answer Me in Movement strategy. Remind them that in that strategy they created gestures in single, original, and unique movements.

2. Share with students that in Movement Strings, their movements will last longer and contain more action before they freeze in their final pose. Consult the *Helpful Terms* (page 210) for movement types, sequences, or ideas to support students' creation of actions. Make sure you introduce the vocabulary as well as model the movements.

3. Read a sequential text with students (or refer to a previously read text), then have them brainstorm a list of the sequence of information or events that occurred in the text.

4. Help students create a movement for each item on the list. Then have them link those series of individual movements together so that they can perform the movements in sequence, similar to beads on a string, one after the other. Remind students, however, that each movement idea is discrete, so the order of the sequence could be rearranged. This will give students the opportunity to learn how altering how information is distributed can alter a narrative's message.

Example:

A student creates a movement for the idea "Connections are built." The student begins crouched down low to the ground with both hands on the ground, then slowly rises while keeping one hand to the floor, as she makes a staircase-like sequence of movements with her other hand getting higher and higher. Her movement concludes with a long stretch connecting the hand on the floor to the hand up in the air, and she looks first down to the hand on the floor and then up to the hand overhead. She decides to do her movement sequence slowly, gradually increasing in speed, while turning in place.

5. Provide each student the opportunity to show their movement to the class, share what the movement represented, and why they made that movement choice. **Note:** We never try to guess what a movement means; rather, this final step in the process gives students the opportunity to verbally share their movement-choice reasoning.

Introducing the Strategies (cont.)

Progressions Introduction

1. Read a simple sequential text with students, such as a nursery rhyme.

2. Instruct students to create a list of how the sequence of events (narrative) or information (nonfiction) is organized in the text (What do we know first? What do we know next?).

3. Ask students to think of how the text uses language, images, or visual support to move readers from one idea to the next. Explain that their focus should be on the transitions between ideas, not just the ideas. Use chart paper to record students' ideas.

4. Explain that inference is a tool that we use in Progressions, which means there is room for interpretation of emotional states when using this strategy.

5. Organize the sequence of events in a two-column chart, as shown in the sample progression chart of "Jack and Jill" on the next page. Explain to students that the left side of the chart details the sequence of events/information from the text. The right side of the chart details the movements that students choose to represent each part of the text. In this strategy, students focus on developing the ideas in column 2 so that the movements flow from one to the next. We avoid static positions, keeping the action going throughout.

6. Have students generate movement ideas for column 2, always linking their movements from what came before to what comes next. Students make their own interpretation about to how to end their progression.

Introducing the Strategies (cont.)

Sample Progression

The example of the nursery rhyme "Jack and Jill" is provided here.

"Jack and Jill" Sequence of Events	Movement Ideas: For Two Students
Jack and Jill went up the hill to fetch a pail of water	Three joyful skips Followed by three cumbersome steps Put hands on thighs and take three labored breaths
Jack fell down and broke his crown	One student stands on one leg and sways Student falls and rolls like a ball to a different place in the room Student ends in a seated position, head in hands
Jill came tumbling after	The next student loses their balance by repeating the same movement that the first student did The student does a rolling movement that takes them to a different place in the room The student ends in seated position, holding their head
End	Students join hands and help each other stand Skip around in a circle Stop and look over their shoulders and shake their heads "no" Hold this final pose to complete the movement progression

Introducing the Strategies (cont.)

Sensory Movement Introduction

1. Explain to students that the Sensory Movement strategy uses the five senses (taste, smell, touch, sight, hearing) to convey information.

2. Explain that in Sensory Movement they will translate the senses into an action. As an example, say: "How would the color red move? Is it big and bold or soft and quiet?" Allow students time to share their ideas about how the color red might move.

3. Also explain that in Sensory Movement they will use their bodies, not their voices, to express the ideas. Ask: "How can we move *like* a screech, instead of screeching?" Have students respond with their ideas.

4. Display the following sentences (or similar sentences appropriate for students):

   ‣ The smell of sweet roses filled the air.
   ‣ The server accidentally dropped the large tray filled with dishes.
   ‣ The car came to a sudden stop.

5. As a class, brainstorm a list of words (or images) from each sentence that fall into any of the five senses and record them on chart paper. Also have students consider motion as another category. **Optional:** Provide students with their own copy of the sentences and have students circle sensory words/ideas that support the brainstormed list.

6. Prompt students to use inferencing skills to add more information to the list. For example, using the sentence "The car came to a sudden stop," they can infer things such as the sound of screeching brakes, the smell of burning rubber, the sight of flashing metal, and the motion of being thrown forward and then caught by the restraint of a seat belt.

7. Have students select a sequence of motions to go with each sentence. They can work individually or in pairs or small groups. Provide students time to share their motion sequences with the class.

Introducing the Strategies (cont.)

Choreographic Structure Introduction

1. Explain to students that a dance suite is a choreographic structure for making longer and more complicated dances than they have made previously. An example of a dance suite is Carol Burch Brown's *Salt Marsh Suite*, which has six sections: tides, water, mud, birds, crabs, and grasses. Each section is its own topic, but all topics fit in the overall concept of the salt marsh.

2. Explain to students that they are going to practice creating a dance suite. They will use five choreographic tools for each of five sections of their dances. Choreographic tools are specific ways that movements can be arranged with one another.

3. Provide students with a theme around which to anchor their movements, such as the ocean, playground games, or animal habitats. If desired, select music to play in the background that matches the theme you select. This also may help students think about different movements they can use.

4. Place students into groups of five. (Groups of four or six also work, depending on the number of students in your class.) Distribute a copy of the *Choreography Planning Guide* (pages 219–222) to each student. Introduce students to each of the five choreographic tools.

5. Explain that the first choreographic tool is called Call and Response. This is when one person (the soloist) performs a movement or movement sequence and then the rest of the group performs that movement or sequence as a response back to the soloist.

6. To practice Call and Response, have one student in each group make some kind of motion and the rest of the group "answer back" with that same motion. If desired, play music while groups practice this choreographic tool. Have students record their movement in the Call and Response section of their planning guide.

7. Explain that the next choreographic tool is called Unison. This is where everyone does the same thing at the same time. Provide groups time to create an action or short movement sequence that they want to do in unison and briefly practice it. Have students record their movement in the Unison section of their planning guide.

8. Have groups put the movements they selected for the first two tools together. First they do their Call and Response movement(s) and then they do the Unison movement(s). Play music during this portion, as desired.

9. Explain that the third choreographic tool that they will learn is called the Fan. This is a sequence of movements where one student does a movement while everyone else is still, then the second person does a movement while everyone else is still, and so on. Have students think of this like a waterfall. In sports arenas, this is similar to the crowd doing the wave. However, in Fan, everyone does their own unique movement.

10. Provide groups time for each student to decide on their Fan movement as well as the order in which they want to do their movements. Have students record their movement in the Fan section of their planning guide.

Introducing the Strategies *(cont.)*

11. Select one group to help model this strategy. To do this, Student A does movement 1, Student B does movement 2, Student C does movement 3, Student D does movement 4, and Student E does movement 5. Then Student E does movement 5 again, then Student D does movement 4, Student C does movement 3, Student B does movement 2, and Student A does movement 1. They arrive back where they started to complete the Fan.

12. Have students practice completing the Fan movement sequence.

13. Have groups put the movements they selected for all three tools together in sequence: Call and Response, Unison, Fan. Play music during this portion, as desired.

14. Explain that the next choreographic tool they will learn is called Rondo. This is when students perform their individual movements in unique sequences, so everyone in the group must learn everyone else's movement. For this practice, have students use the same movements they did in Fan, but have them teach them all to each other.

15. Display the Movement Sequence Guide shown on the next page to show how each student performs the movement sequence in a different order, but everyone is moving at the same time. Whereas in Unison everyone is doing the same thing at the same time, in Rondo it is similar to a round.

16. Have students record their movements in the Rondo section of their planning guide. Provide students time to practice.

17. Have groups put the movements they selected for all four tools together in sequence: Call and Response, Unison, Fan, Rondo. Play music during this portion, as desired.

18. Explain that the last choreographic tool students will learn is called Recurrence. This is the repetition of something that has been done before, but usually with a slight twist.

19. Have groups select a movement or movement sequence they have already done and then put a creative twist on it. For example, if students swayed their hands in the air earlier, this time they could sway their hands in the air while turning in a circle. Provide students time to practice their selected movement. Have them record their movement in the Recurrence section of their planning guide.

20. Have groups put all the movements for all five tools together in sequence: Call and Response, Unison, Fan, Rondo, Recurrence. Play music during this portion, as desired.

21. If desired, give each group time to share their dance suite with the rest of the class. This could be further developed into a school assembly.

Consider breaking up the introduction to the strategies over three to four days so that students feel comfortable with each choreographic tool before moving on.

Introducing the Strategies (cont.)

Movement Sequence Guide

Student A Sequence	Student B Sequence	Student C Sequence	Student D Sequence	Student E Sequence
1	2	3	4	5
2	3	4	5	1
3	4	5	1	2
4	5	1	2	3
5	1	2	3	4

Name: _____ Date: _____

Choreography Planning Guide

Directions: Work with your group to select a movement or movement sequence for each choreographic tool. Draw or describe the movements, and think about and respond to the questions provided.

Call and Response: One student performs a movement or movement sequence, and then the group performs that movement or sequence as a response back to the student.

Draw a diagram that describes how you will use Call and Response.

Who will be the "caller"? Will the caller always be the same?

What is the formation (circles, lines, or random)? Will the formation always be the same?

Creative Movement

Choreography Planning Guide (cont.)

Unison: Everyone is doing the same thing at the same time.

Draw or describe the movement that everyone will learn.

Fan: One person does a movement while everyone else is still, then the second person does a movement while everyone else is still, and so on. Each student gets a turn, then the movements are completed in reverse order.

Draw a diagram that shows the order of everyone in the Fan. Describe each person's movement(s).

Name: _____ Date: _____

Choreography Planning Guide *(cont.)*

Rondo: You will perform your individual movements in unique sequences, so everyone in the group must learn everyone else's movement(s).

Draw or describe each person's movement(s).

Name: _____ Date: _____

Choreography Planning Guide (cont.)

Use the chart to record the order in which each person will perform the movements.

Student A Sequence	Student B Sequence	Student C Sequence	Student D Sequence	Student E Sequence

Recurrence: This is the repetition of something that has been done before, but usually with a slight twist.

Select one of the choreographic tools and plan to repeat it, but with a twist! What will that twist be?

Answer Me in Movement

Model Lesson: *Living Sunlight* Answer Me in Movement

Overview

In this lesson, students read the book *Living Sunlight: How Plants Bring the Earth to Life* by Molly Bang and Penny Chisholm and use the Answer Me in Movement strategy to reflect on how humans get energy from plants and the photosynthesis process. The sample teacher and student dialogue is not intended to be prescriptive; rather, it is meant to guide your thinking and model how the strategy may play out.

Materials

▸ *Living Sunlight: How Plants Bring the Earth to Life* by Molly Bang and Penny Chisholm

▸ *Elements of Creative Movement* (page 207)

▸ *Helpful Terms* (page 210)

▸ chart paper

Standards

Grades K–2

▸ Conducts an investigation to determine if plants need sunlight and water to grow

▸ Describes how words and phrases (regular beats, alliteration, rhymes, repeated lines) supply rhythm and meaning in a story, poem, or song

▸ Explores movement inspired by a variety of stimuli and identifies the source

Grades 3–5

▸ Describes how energy and fuels are derived from natural resources and their uses affect the environment

▸ Determines the meaning of words and phrases in a text, including figurative language such as metaphors and similes

▸ Experiments with a variety of self-identified stimuli for movement

Grades 6–8

▸ Constructs a scientific explanation based on evidence for the role of photosynthesis in the cycling of matter and flow of energy into and out of organisms

▸ Determines the meaning of words and phrases in a text, including figurative and connotative meanings; analyzes the impact of word choices on meaning and tone

▸ Relates similar or contrasting ideas to develop choreography using a variety of stimuli

Grades 9–12

▸ Uses a model to describe how variations in the flow of energy into and out of Earth's systems result in changes in climate

▸ Determines the meaning of words and phrases in a text, including figurative and connotative meanings; analyzes the impact of word choices on meaning and tone

▸ Explores a variety of stimuli for sourcing movement to develop a dance study

Answer Me in Movement (cont.)

Preparation

Have students practice using the Answer Me in Movement strategy (page 211) before beginning this lesson. This activity is best done in a circle to make it is easy to move the turn from next person to next person without having to call on anyone, or prioritizing order. The circle is a democratizing practice that gives everyone a turn. Additional suggestions are provided in the Specific Grade-Level Ideas.

Procedure

1. Read aloud the book *Living Sunlight: How Plants Bring the Earth to Life*. After completing the book, reread the page that begins, "But wait! You are not green!" and read through to the page that ends, "You share life with everything alive."

2. Display the illustrations from that same section of the book. Ask students what ideas in the illustrations may not be as fully presented in the words alone. Share that when we use movement, we also use inferencing and prior knowledge to show things that aren't in a text.

3. After reading and discussing those pages in detail, ask students the question from the book: "So, how do YOU get energy from sunlight? Do you know?"

4. Arrange students in a circle. Remind students how to respond after a clap for the Answer Me in Movement strategy.

5. Say to students, "When I clap, answer me in movement; show me with movement, not with words, one way that you get your energy from the sun and photosynthesis." Explain that it is all right to have the same response as someone else, and it also is all right to have a unique choice.

6. Suggest that students think of their movement in three parts. "What is your beginning pose? What is the motion that happens? What is your ending pose? We will all begin together, but some people's movement might last a little longer than someone else's, so when you finish, end by staying frozen in your final pose. Wait until everyone is done, then I will clap and we can all relax our final positions." Here are some examples of how a student might answer in movement:

   - Student has decided that we get energy from eating vegetables. They cup their hands together, making a leafy structure, then they put their face into their hands and pantomime eating. They freeze in the eating gesture.

   - Student has decided that the picture of the sloth hanging upside down eating from the tree is their answer. They begin by leaning sideways, trying to resemble being upside down, and then they bring their little sloth hands to their mouth and freeze in the leaning over/hand to mouth position.

   - Student has decided that the oxygen that plants breathe out is their response. They begin by stretching their arms out to the side, then hug their arms into themselves, make a little shaking movement, then cup their hands and blow air out as if blowing out a candle.

7. Go around the circle and have students take turns showing their movements. When one student has finished, the next student takes a turn.

Option: Add music (without lyrics) and let students do the movement sequence to music.

Answer Me in Movement (cont.)

8. Go around the circle a second time. With this round, have students show their movements again and then tell the class what they were thinking and why they chose their movement to express their ideas about how we get energy.

9. Reread the portion of text that says, "So you see? Life keeps circling around and round on your planet." Tell students that they will now do their movements one after another, in the circle, without talking. Remind students to be aware when the person before them has finished, and then it is their turn. This will imitate the feeling of the circle of life moving around them.

10. Highlight how each student made a unique choice—although some may have been similar, each student's choice is unique. Tell students, "This is how we are as a community of life. There are many parts of what keeps life on Earth, from plants to animals to humans."

11. Debrief this lesson, using the Discussion Questions.

Discussion Questions

- How is getting your message across with movement different from communicating with words?

- How can movement be an effective communication tool?

- In what ways is movement similar to illustrations in a book?

Specific Grade Level Ideas

Grades K–2

Identify weather terminology to be explored through movement such as *cloud cover, precipitation,* and so on. Name a weather term and ask students, "Answer me in movement: What is <weather term>?"

Grades 3–5

Following an exploration of light illuminating objects in the dark, ask students, "Answer me in movement: What is a light wave?"

Grades 6–8

After studying what scientists have discovered about hereditary traits, ask students, "Answer me in movement: What is a genetic trait?"

Grades 9–12

Engage students in listing the bulk properties of matter such as *melting point, boiling point, vapor, surface tension,* and so on. For each term, ask students, "Answer me in movement: What is <term>?"

Movement Strings

Model Lesson: *Living Sunlight* Movement Strings

Overview

In this lesson, students work with the book *Living Sunlight: How Plants Bring the Earth to Life* by Molly Bang and Penny Chisholm and use the Movement Strings strategy to identify the effects of sun's energy on Earth. Students create individual movements and then link them to form a sequence of movements to communicate the sequential order of the ideas.

Materials

▸ *Living Sunlight: How Plants Bring the Earth to Life* by Molly Bang and Penny Chisholm

▸ chart paper

▸ *Elements of Creative Movement* (page 207)

▸ *Helpful Terms* (page 210)

Standards

Grades K–2

▸ Conducts an investigation to determine if plants need sunlight and water to grow

▸ Describes how words and phrases (for example, regular beats, alliteration, rhymes, repeated lines) supply rhythm and meaning in a story, poem, or song

▸ Chooses movements that express a main idea or emotion, or follow a musical phrase

Grades 3–5

▸ Describes how energy and fuels are derived from natural resources and their uses affect the environment

▸ Determines the meaning of words and phrases used in a text, including figurative language such as metaphors and similes

▸ Develops a dance phrase that expresses and communicates an idea or feeling

Grades 6–8

▸ Constructs a scientific explanation based on evidence for the role of photosynthesis in the cycling of matter and flow of energy into and out of organisms

▸ Determines the meaning of words and phrases in a text, including figurative and connotative meanings; analyzes the impact of word choices on meaning and tone

▸ Implements movement from a variety of stimuli to develop content for an original dance

Grades 9–12

▸ Uses a model to describe how variations in the flow of energy into and out of Earth's systems result in changes in climate

▸ Determines the meaning of words and phrases in a text, including figurative and connotative meanings; analyzes the impact of word choices on meaning and tone

▸ Explores a variety of stimuli for sourcing movement to develop a dance study

Movement Strings (cont.)

Preparation

Have students practice using the Movement Strings strategy (page 212) before beginning this lesson. Additionally, this strategy builds on what was learned from the Answer Me in Movement strategy. If students are not familiar with that strategy, practice it with them first before beginning Movement Strings. Additional suggestions are provided in the Specific Grade-Level Ideas.

Procedure

1. Review the book *Living Sunlight: How Plants Bring the Earth to Life*. Reread the pages that begin, "I am your sun, your golden star" and end, "I do all this, but I do far, far more."

2. Ask students what sunlight does for Earth. Record students' ideas on chart paper. Have students go back to the text as well as use their own background knowledge to create the list of ideas. (Ideas from the text include "warming the land and seas, melting glaciers, and creating winds." The "Notes" page of the book also has additional information, if needed.)

3. Decide whether you would like students to work individually, in pairs, or in small groups. If students work individually, have them select one to three ideas from the brainstormed list to turn into a movement string. If they work in pairs or groups of three, have them select three to five ideas. And if they work in groups of four or five, have them select four to six ideas. **Note:** For younger students, you can choose to do this as a whole group instead.

4. Have students brainstorm a movement idea for each item on their list. Explain that the movement ideas must include everyone in the group.

Examples:

- **Warm the land:** Students form a circle and hold hands; they lift their arms up, then bring them down to the ground while moving the circle in a clockwise direction.

- **Warm the sea:** Students do the same movement as above, except this time they wave their arms up and down like waves in the ocean.

- **Melt glaciers:** Students form a human sculpture that resembles a glacier with jagged arm and leg angles. First one student's head droops (melts), while the second student droops (melts) their back, and the third begins to bend in their knees. This gradual drooping/melting occurs until all students are in a low-level (close to the ground) shape that resembles a lake.

- **Create winds:** Students move as if blown by the wind throughout the room.

- **Cause plants to grow:** From individual spots in the room, each student curls up in a tight ball like a seed. They gradually "grow" taller and taller.

5. Once groups have decided on their movements, have them practice "stringing" them together to create a movement string. Groups should practice their movement strings until they have memorized them and feel comfortable with the sequence of motions. The string represents the different ways the sun affects Earth.

6. Have groups perform their movement strings for the rest of the class. If desired, play music without lyrics during each performance. When each group performs, let the music play as atmosphere. When groups present their movement strings, have students wait in stillness until they

Movement Strings (cont.)

hear the music. When they are done, students come to stillness and wait for you to fade the music before they relax. This heightens the awareness of the movement.

7. Have the class observe the movement presentations closely and identify the ideas being portrayed as well as the movement choices that were most compelling. Use the Discussion Questions to further debrief each movement string presentation.

Discussion Questions

▸ How did creating movement ideas, or watching the ideas of others, challenge you to think differently about the effect of the sun's energy on Earth?

▸ Do you have any new questions about "how" something might happen because of the sun's energy? For instance, do you wonder how the sun's energy creates wind?

▸ What connections did you notice between your artistic choices and the science content you explored?

▸ What did you notice in the dances created by others that illuminated your thinking about the sun's effect on Earth or about the power of dance to communicate ideas?

Specific Grade-Level Ideas

Grades K–2

Make a list of three to five simple machines. Ask students to create movement ideas for each item on the list. Then have them put them together to make a movement string. Remind students that a movement string is like a list—it is not a sequence or an enactment.

Grades 3–5

Create small groups and have each group think of three to five ideas of where water is found on Earth (remind them that water can be solid or liquid). Have students brainstorm a movement for each idea and sequence them together to form a movement string.

Grades 6–8

Ask students to identify what they know about stars, or any other astronomical topic such as planets, black holes, or meteors. Have students make a list of five to six ideas, create a movement idea for each one, and link them together as a movement string.

Grades 9–12

Have small groups of students think about the forces of motion. Have each group make a list of ideas about the forces of motion and create a movement for each idea. Ask students to create a movement string from that list.

Progressions

Model Lesson: *Living Sunlight* Progressions

Overview

Progressions are like movement strings, in that movements are put together in a sequential sequence; but in progressions students focus on the emotional development and transitions of how one thing evolves into the next. The Progressions strategy is particularly useful in science to understand the steps of a process. In this lesson, students focus on the process of photosynthesis, using the book *Living Sunlight: How Plants Bring the Earth to Life* by Molly Bang and Penny Chisholm.

Materials

▸ *Living Sunlight: How Plants Bring the Earth to Life* by Molly Bang and Penny Chisholm

▸ *Elements of Creative Movement* (page 207)

▸ *Helpful Terms* (page 210)

Standards

Grades K–2

▸ Conducts an investigation to determine if plants need sunlight and water to grow

▸ Describes the connection between two individuals, events, or ideas in a text

▸ Chooses movements that express a main idea or emotion, or follow a musical phrase

Grades 3–5

▸ Describes how energy and fuels are derived from natural resources and their uses affect the environment

▸ Describes the relationship between historical events, scientific ideas, or steps in technical procedures, using language that pertains to time, sequence, and cause/effect

▸ Develops a dance phrase that expresses and communicates an idea or feeling

Grades 6–8

▸ Constructs a scientific explanation based on evidence for the role of photosynthesis in the cycling of matter and flow of energy into and out of organisms

▸ Analyzes in detail how a key individual, event, or idea is introduced and elaborated in a text

▸ Implements movement from a variety of stimuli to develop content for an original dance

Grades 9–12

▸ Uses a model to describe how variations in the flow of energy into and out of Earth's systems result in changes in climate

▸ Analyzes how the author unfolds a series of ideas or events, including how they are introduced and developed, and the connections drawn between them

▸ Explores a variety of stimuli for sourcing movement to develop a dance study

Progressions (cont.)

Preparation

Have students practice using the Progressions strategy (page 213) before beginning this lesson. Additionally, this strategy builds on what was learned from the Answer Me in Movement and Movement Strings strategies. If students are not familiar with those strategies, practice them first before beginning this Progressions strategy. Additional suggestions are provided in the Specific Grade Level Ideas.

Procedure

1. Review the book *Living Sunlight: How Plants Bring the Earth to Life* with students. Read aloud the pages that begin, "Your secret starts in plants . . ." and end, "This is my gift of energy to you."

2. As a class, study the text and the illustrations on the first page spread referenced in step 1. Discuss the four boxes in the illustration and what the illustrator is representing in those drawings.

3. Direct students to the next page spread and the box shown there. Discuss how the illustration demonstrates the ideas of the text on the spread. Then look at the illustration on the third page spread. Ask students what the words and illustration tell them about plants building "all their parts." Explain how this entire process—photosynthesis—is how life is made with sunlight.

4. Divide the class into small groups. Using the five boxes, the final full illustration, and the text descriptions, have groups write a caption for each box and the final page in their own words. They should have six "captions" that describe the phases of photosynthesis.

5. Have groups create a movement idea for each caption they wrote. Explain that even though the illustrations are static

(not moving), because the students are using movement, they can "animate" each illustration. Remind students to not only think about a movement for each phase of photosynthesis, but also consider how they want to transition from one movement to the next. Use the Planning Questions to support students as they work.

6. If needed, support students by creating a table or prompt list to help them organize their thoughts, such as the following:

Caption 1:	Transition:	Movements:
Caption 2:	Transition:	Movements:
Caption 3:	Transition:	Movements:
Caption 4:	Transition:	Movements:
Caption 5:	Transition:	Movements:
Caption 6:	Transition:	Movements:

7. Once groups have decided on their movements that carry them through the phases of photosynthesis and transitions, have groups rehearse and memorize their movements so they can perform their completed progressions for the rest of the class.

8. Allow groups time to share their progressions with the rest of the class.

9. Debrief, using the Discussion Questions.

Progressions (cont.)

Planning Questions

▸ How will you show that phase of photosynthesis with your body?

▸ How will you best communicate the action by making thoughtful transitions that engage the viewer emotionally?

▸ When you get to the end of that movement idea, what will the transition be from this phase to the next phase?

▸ Is the transition a quick shift? Does it happen gradually? Does everyone change at the same time, or does it move through the group?

▸ Does the transition move to another part of the room/performance area?

Discussion Questions

▸ How did movement help us understand photosynthesis, either by watching the dance progressions or from your own dance progression?

▸ How does a writer keep the reader's interest through the use of transitions?

▸ How do transitions make you feel like you are part of the unfolding of the process?

Specific Grade Level Ideas

Grades K–2

Have students identify each step in the life cycle of a dandelion. Create a movement for each step and have them show in movement how each stage progresses to the next. Because this is a cyclical process, students can discuss where to begin and where to end.

Grades 3–5

Ask students to make a list of how water is distributed in the environment. Identify how environmental changes affect water quality such as how storm water runoff affects streams, rivers, and lakes.

Have students create a movement for each environmental change and sequence them in order, paying attention to the transitions between each step. At the conclusion, students will have a movement progression dance for environmental health of the water, including challenges and solutions.

Grades 6–8

Divide the class into small groups. Have each group choose a law of motion. Have students create a movement for the process of their law of motion, paying attention to the transitions between each part of the process. At the conclusion, students will have a movement progression dance that demonstrates the law of motion.

Grades 9–12

With students, examine the processes of mitosis and meiosis. Divide the class into small groups. Have students create a movement for each part of the cell division process and sequence them in order, paying attention to the transitions between each step. At the conclusion, students will have a movement progression dance for the process of both types of cell division.

Sensory Movement

Model Lesson: *Living Sunlight* Sensory Movement

Overview

Using the book *Living Sunlight: How Plants Bring the Earth to Life,* readers examine the text and the illustrations to see how sensorial imagery is used to communicate information about photosynthesis. Students explore this sensory imagery by drawing on science and their own experiences of the natural world, translating the rich details into movements. All five senses are used for sensory exploration, with "motion" included as a sixth sense. In sensory movement, we become aware of how language uses sensorial words to communicate by evoking our sensory experiences.

Materials

‣ *Living Sunlight: How Plants Bring the Earth to Life* by Molly Bang and Penny Chisholm

‣ *Sensory Movement Chart* (page 237)

‣ *Elements of Creative Movement* (page 207)

‣ *Helpful Terms* (page 210)

Standards

Grades K–2

‣ Conducts an investigation to determine if plants need sunlight and water to grow

‣ Identifies words and phrases in stories or poems that suggest feelings or appeal to the senses

‣ Explores movement inspired by a variety of stimuli and suggests additional sources for movement ideas

Grades 3–5

‣ Describes how energy and fuels are derived from natural resources and their uses affect the environment

‣ Determines the meaning of words and phrases as they are used in a text, distinguishing literal from nonliteral language

‣ Builds content for choreography using several stimuli

Grades 6–8

‣ Constructs a scientific explanation based on evidence for the role of photosynthesis in the cycling of matter and flow of energy into and out of organisms

‣ Determines the meaning of words and phrases in a text, including figurative and connotative meanings; analyzes the impact of word choices on meaning and tone

‣ Relates similar or contrasting ideas to develop choreography using a variety of stimuli

Grades 9–12

‣ Uses a model to describe how variations in the flow of energy into and out of Earth's systems result in changes in climate

‣ Determines the meaning of words and phrases in the text, including figurative and connotative meanings; analyzes the impact of word choices on meaning and tone

‣ Explores a variety of stimuli for sourcing movement to develop a dance study

Sensory Movement (cont.)

Preparation

Have students practice using the Sensory Movement strategy (page 215) before beginning this lesson. Additionally, this strategy builds on what students learned from the Answer Me in Movement, Movement Strings, and Progressions strategies. If students are not familiar with those strategies, practice them first before beginning this Sensory Movement strategy. Additional suggestions are provided in the Specific Grade-Level Ideas.

Procedure

1. Reread *Living Sunlight: How Plants Bring the Earth to Life* by Molly Bang and Penny Chisholm. Direct students to the pages in the book that begin, "Breathe in. Feel the oxygen flow into your nose, your mouth—all through your body" and to the page that ends, "They will use it to build more sugar—food for themselves and other living things."

2. Share with students that you will be using some of the directions from the text to focus their breathing and complete a breathing exercise. Have students find a quiet space to sit or lie down inside the classroom, or, if preferred, take students outside.

3. Explain that students are going to try a simple breathing pattern known as the square. To do this, have students breathe in gently through the nose for four counts, hold gently for four counts, exhale softly through gently pursed lips for four counts, and hold gently for four counts. They can close their eyes or just look down with a soft focus. Instruct students to focus on breathing in that same breathing pattern while they listen to you slowly read the following:

   As you breathe in, feel the oxygen flow into your nose, your lungs—all through your body.

   As you breathe out, imagine that you are breathing out carbon dioxide that the plants all breathe in.

4. Allow five minutes for this quiet breathing exercise. Gently repeat the prompt from step 3 several times throughout the five minutes. If desired, have soft music playing in the background.

5. After the breathing exercise, explain to students that sensory language is language that uses the five senses: sight, taste, sound, touch, and smell. For this strategy, share with students that they also want to consider motion as a sixth sense, but motion words can carry sensorial images with them. For example, cutting flowers from a bush has the action of cutting and a sound and a smell to go with it.

6. Instruct students to take a silent walk around the school grounds as a class. Explain that without talking, students will use their six senses to observe the world around them. They must pay attention to what they can see, hear, and smell. They should observe the motion around them, such as how a bird travels across the sky or how a breeze moves. They may gently touch things around them to activate their tactile senses. Also explain that to experience taste, they will all begin with a sip of water.

7. As students come back into the classroom, before saying a word, have them make a list of five things they experienced for each of the six senses.

8. Display the page from *Living Sunlight* that begins, "So you see? Life keeps circling round and round on your planet Earth, through photosynthesis, and through yourselves. You share life with everything alive."

Sensory Movement (cont.)

9. Distribute copies of the *Sensory Movement Chart*. Direct students to choose one item from each of their lists that ties back to how photosynthesis plays a part in their existence. Students can do this individually, as a class, or in small groups.

10. Have students work in groups to complete the *Sensory Movement Chart*. Explain that they should turn each of the selected ideas in column 1 into movement to express how photosynthesis is used in the sensory choice. The table below shows some ideas.

11. Once groups complete their charts, explain that they must order the movements together so that they can perform them one after another. Rehearse and memorize your movements so you can perform them for the class without a pause or break, moving continuously from one idea to the next.

12. After each group has created and practiced their sensory movements, provide time for each group to show it to the rest of the class.

13. Use the Discussion Questions to debrief with students after each group shares.

Item from Sensory List	Makes Me Think of Photosynthesis . . .	Movement Idea
Sight: Dandelion	Plants breathe out oxygen and breathe in carbon dioxide.	Make a shape like a dandelion, and breathe in, gathering my arms around myself, and then exhale, opening my arms and turning in a circle.
Sound: A bird call	Birds get their energy from eating berries from plants.	Make circular movements with the arms, then curve into the center of my body, causing an energetic trembling through my body.
Touch: The feeling of the sun on my skin	The sun radiates heat and light in all directions; some of it comes to Earth.	Start in a low ball shape; as I stand, I expand outward like a radiating sun, casting that light and energy not only toward the sky, but to the sides and down to the ground as well.

Sensory Movement *(cont.)*

Discussion Questions

▸ How did the movements make you aware of photosynthesis in the world around you?

▸ How does a writer use sensory words and motion words to create interest?

▸ What did you learn about sensory words by translating them into movement? For example, what did it feel like to do a sound word without the sound?

▸ What did you love about what you saw? Why?

▸ Was there anything that this group did that gave you an idea of something you would like to use in your next sensory movement?

▸ If you were to keep working on this sensory movement exercise, what would you add, take away, or change?

Sensory Movement (cont.)

Specific Grade-Level Ideas

Grades K–2

Invite students to investigate the characteristics of a weather event or condition. As a whole class or in small groups, have students choose one event or condition and try to describe it using the five senses. For example, "What does rain smell like?" Translate the answer into movement. Continue on for all five senses, then perform them in a sequence.

Grades 3–5

Have students examine the differences between young animals and their parents. Divide the class into small groups, and have each group choose a specific animal. Then have groups compare the babies and parents by identifying what changes over time and making comparisons using their senses. Here are some questions for students to consider: "What do the animals look like? Sound like? How does the quality of the fur/body change? How are the babies and parents alike? How are they different?" Have students create a movement sequence based on the young animal and another for the adult animal. Help students pay attention to how this is a compare/contrast exercise.

Grades 6–8

Divide the class into small groups and ask them to consider how sound waves travel through different mediums. Have students use sensory imagery and language to express how a sound wave travels differently through air, the earth, or other mediums. Challenge students to create a movement for each sensorial descriptor and sequence the movements together. Have students perform their movement sequences in small groups or in front of the class.

Grades 9–12

Divide the class into small groups. Have each group use sensory language and imagery to show, in movement, each nuclear process: fusion, fission, and radioactive decay. Students should pay specific attention to how the release and absorption of energy functions in each process and how that energy release and absorption is sensorially motivated.

Name: _____ Date: _____

Sensory Movement Chart

Directions: Record one idea from each list of sensory ideas from the silent walk. Write about how that idea connects to photosynthesis, and record a movement that illustrates that idea. An example is shown below.

Item from Sensory List	Makes Me Think of Photosynthesis . . .	Movement Idea
Example **Sight:** dandelion	Plants breathe out oxygen and breathe in carbon dioxide.	Make a shape like a dandelion, and breathe in, gathering my arms around myself, and then exhale, opening my arms and turning in a circle.
Sight:		
Sound:		
Tactile:		
Taste:		
Smell:		
Motion:		

Choreographic Structure

Model Lesson: *Living Sunlight* Choreography

Overview

For each previous creative movement strategy (Answer Me in Movement, Movement Strings, Progressions, and Sensory Movement), students essentially choreographed short creative movement dances. In this strategy, students generate movement ideas based on photosynthesis, develop those ideas using choreographic tools, and place them in the choreographic structure known as a suite. Students are introduced to choreographic tools and how to create overall more complex choreography.

Materials

- *Living Sunlight: How Plants Bring the Earth to Life* by Molly Bang and Penny Chisholm
- *Living Sunlight Movement Chart* (page 243)
- *Living Sunlight Choreography Planning Guide* (pages 244–248)
- *Elements of Creative Movement* (page 207)
- *Helpful Terms* (page 210)

Standards

Grades K–2

- Conducts an investigation to determine if plants need sunlight and water to grow
- Participates in conversations with peers and adults in small and larger groups
- Demonstrates a range of movements, body patterning, and dance sequences that require moving through space using a variety of pathways

Grades 3–5

- Describes how energy and fuels are derived from natural resources and their uses affect the environment
- Engages in discussions with diverse partners, building on others' ideas and expressing their own clearly
- Recalls and executes a series of dance phrases using fundamental dance skills

Grades 6–8

- Constructs a scientific explanation based on evidence for the role of photosynthesis in the cycling of matter and flow of energy into and out of organisms
- Engages in discussions with diverse partners, building on others' ideas and expressing their own clearly
- Embodies technical dance skills to replicate, recall, and execute spatial designs and musical or rhythmical dance phrases

Grades 9–12

- Uses a model to describe how variations in the flow of energy into and out of Earth's systems result in changes in climate
- Engages in discussions with diverse partners, building on others' ideas and expressing their own clearly and persuasively
- Embodies technical dance skills to retain and execute dance choreography

Choreographic Structure (cont.)

Preparation

Have students practice using the Choreographic Structure (page 216) before beginning this lesson. Additionally, this strategy builds on what was learned from the Answer Me in Movement, Movement Strings, Progressions, and Sensory Movement strategies. If students are not familiar with those strategies, practice them first before beginning the Choreography strategy. Review the Planning Questions ahead of time so you are able to prompt students/groups as needed throughout the entire lesson. Additional suggestions are provided in the Specific Grade-Level Ideas.

Procedure

1. Explain to students that they are going to use the process of photosynthesis to create an entire group of movements that celebrates light, energy, and how plants bring the earth to life. This is called a dance suite.

2. Distribute copies of the *Living Sunlight Movement Chart*. Review the steps of photosynthesis outlined in the text:

   1. Plants suck up water from the earth.

   2. In daylight, plants catch the sun's energy with chlorophyll.

   3. Kazap! Plants use energy to break apart the water into hydrogen and oxygen.

   4. As the plants break apart the water, the sun's energy is trapped in little packets.

   5. Plants breathe out the oxygen.

   6. And plants breathe in carbon dioxide from the air.

   7. Plants use the packets of energy, and the carbon dioxide to build sugar.

   8. Plants use the sugar to build their parts and stay alive.

   9. Humans and animals eat plants and so have their energy from the Sun and the work of the plants.

The nine steps mirror the text *Living Sunlight: How Plants Bring the Earth to Life.* Modify the number of steps or the complexity of the information in each step to best meet the needs of students.

3. Divide the class into small groups of four to five.

4. Have groups complete the *Living Sunlight Movement Chart*. Remind them that for each movement(s) they choose for each step in the photosynthesis process, they should feel confident they can repeat it. If needed, allow students to use words and drawings to help them remember each movement. Here are some movement ideas:

Plants suck up water from the earth: Start with hands over heart; right arm makes big circle to the side, then left stretches out to the other side; end with a jump.

In daylight, plants catch the sun's energy with chlorophyll: Start with hands on opposite shoulders; open the right arm out in front and then the left; end with a turn.

Kazap! Plants use energy to break apart the water into hydrogen and oxygen. Start with right hand at shoulder height; make a movement like a wave going across the body; end by clapping hands together.

As the plants break apart the water, the sun's energy is trapped in little packets: Start with hands on hips; then reach out to one side then the other side; end by clasping both hands together in a handshake.

Plants breathe out the oxygen: Start with hands on top of head; then as if untying a long braid, loosen imaginary hair like a waterfall flowing down; end by making a "shhh" gesture over the lips.

Choreographic Structure *(cont.)*

5. Provide students with time to practice each movement in the photosynthesis process.

6. Distribute a copy of the *Living Sunlight Choreography Planning Guide* to each student. Explain that they are going to use five different choreographic tools—Call and Response, Unison, Fan, Rondo, and Recurrence—to create a dance suite to celebrate the process of photosynthesis and how plants bring the earth to life.

Call and Response

1. Remind students that Call and Response is when one person (the soloist) performs a movement or movement sequence, and then the rest of the group performs that movement or sequence as a response back to the soloist.

2. Explain to students that they will use all nine movements they selected for the steps of photosynthesis to create their Call and Response.

3. Prompt students to consider formation for the Call and Response. Is the caller in the center of a circle, with the responders around them? Or does the caller stand in front of the responders in a row? Will just one person be the caller, or will different students have a turn? Have students record information about their formation in their *Living Sunlight Choreography Planning Guide*.

4. Allow students time to practice this until they can perform it with confidence.

Unison

1. Remind students that the choreographic tool Unison is used when all members of the group are doing the same thing at the same time in a continual flow from beginning to end.

2. Explain that students will use all nine movements they selected for the steps of photosynthesis, but they need to decide in what order they want to perform the movements and in what formation.

3. Have students record information about their sequence and formation in their *Living Sunlight Choreography Planning Guide*.

4. Allow students time to practice this until they can perform it with confidence.

Fan

1. Remind students that a Fan is a sequence of movements in which one person does a movement while everyone else is still, then the second person does a movement while everyone else is still, and so on. Explain that it is similar to the wave at a sports arena, except everyone is doing their own unique movement.

2. Explain to students that they will use all nine movements they selected for the steps of photosynthesis, but they need to decide in what order they want to perform the movements and in what formation. For example:

   Formation: Students make a single line facing the audience, one behind the other from shortest to tallest

   Action:

   Student A does movement 1, then freezes.
   Student B does movement 2, then freezes.
   Student C does movement 3, then freezes.
   Student D does movement 4, then freezes.
   Student E does movement 5, then freezes.
   Student D does movement 6, then freezes.
   Student C does movement 7, then freezes.
   Student B does movement 8, then freezes.
   Student A does movement 9, then freezes.

 © Shell Education

Choreographic Structure (cont.)

3. Explain to students that the Fan should happen as smoothly as possible, so when one movement ends, the next student's movement comes fairly quickly afterward.

4. Have students record information about their sequence and formation in their *Living Sunlight Choreography Planning Guide*.

5. Allow students time to practice this until they can perform their sequence with confidence.

Rondo

1. Remind students that in Rondo, each student performs the sequence in a different order, but all at the same time.

2. Explain to students that they will use all nine movements they selected for the steps of photosynthesis, but they need to decide in what order they want to perform the movements and in what formation. Have students use the table on their *Living Sunlight Choreography Planning Guide* to create the movement sequence for each person in their group.

   Example:

   Student A: 1, 2, 3, 4, 5, 6, 7, 8, 9
   Student B: 2, 3, 4, 5, 6, 7, 8, 9, 1
   Student C: 3, 4, 5, 6, 7, 8, 9, 1, 2
   Student D: 4, 5, 6, 7, 8, 9, 1, 2, 3
   Student E: 5, 6, 7, 8, 9, 1, 2, 3, 4

3. As students decide how they want to perform the sequences, explain that their goal is to work on timing so that even though each person's sequence is different, everyone begins and ends the Rondo at the same time.

4. Allow students time to practice until they can perform these movements with confidence.

Unison with Recurrence

1. Explain to students that they will use the choreographic tool of Unison and Recurrence for the last section of their dance suite. Remind them that Recurrence is the repetition of something that has been done before, but usually with a slight twist.

2. Explain that they will use the same Unison technique and movements from earlier. Have groups work together to decide what kinds of twists they want to put on the original movements.

3. Once groups have decided on their movements, have them record the information in their *Living Sunlight Choreography Planning Guide*.

4. Allow students time to practice until they perform these movements with confidence.

Putting It Together

1. Explain to students that now it is time to put everything together into one full performance.

2. Allow groups time to review all the movements and practice them in sequence.

Choreographic Structure (cont.)

This collection of dance suites could be performed for a whole school assembly. To do this, assign a student, or teacher, to read the text aloud to the audience. After the audience has listened to the text, each group performs. It may be helpful to use music as background as well.

Planning Questions

▸ What formation will the five students in the group take in relationship to one another? You could all be in a circle, in two rows facing the audience, in a single line facing the audience, in a random pattern, and so on. Draw various formations that dancers could make. Use a dot to represent each dancer. You can do this on individual paper or come to the board and share an idea.

   Example: dancers could all be in a circle

   Example: dancers could be in two rows

   Example: dancers could be lined up behind one another

   Example: dancers could be scattered randomly

▸ Will the movements all be done in one place, or will the movements cause the dancer to move from one location to another? In dance, this is called "traveling" or "locomotion." You could walk, skip, run, crawl, or leap to get from one place to another. It's up to you!

▸ The dance suite form is in distinct sections, but what kinds of transitions will link all the sections together? How will the dancers get from one formation to another?

Specific Grade-Level Ideas

Grades K–2

Choose a theme for the dance suite such as how the shape of an object (for example, a wheel) helps it function.

Grades 3–5

Choose a theme for the dance suite such as patterns in a natural and human-designed world.

Grades 6-8

Choose a theme for the dance suite such as genetic variations and mutations due to environmental impact.

Grades 9–12

Choose a theme for the dance suite such as the relationship between DNA and chromosomes.

Name: _____ Date: _____

Living Sunlight Movement Chart

Directions: Work with your group. Draw or describe the movements you select for each step in the process of photosynthesis.

Step	Photosynthesis Step Description	Movement Description
1	Plants suck up water from the earth.	
2	In daylight, plants catch the sun's energy with chlorophyll.	
3	Kazap! Plants use energy to break apart the water into hydrogen and oxygen.	
4	As the plants break apart the water, the sun's energy is trapped in little packets.	
5	Plants breathe out the oxygen.	
6	And plants breathe in carbon dioxide from the air.	
7	Plants use the packets of energy and the carbon dioxide to build sugar.	
8	Plants use the sugar to build their parts and stay alive.	
9	Humans and animals eat plants, and so have their energy from the sun and the work of the plants.	

Name: _____ Date: _____

Living Sunlight Choreography Planning Guide

Directions: Read the information in each box and follow the directions from your teacher. Draw or describe the movements you and your group select for each choreographic tool.

Call and Response

Use the movements from the steps of photosynthesis.

Draw a diagram that describes how you will use Call and Response.

Who will be the "caller"? Will the caller always be the same?

What is the formation (circles, lines, random)? Will the formation always be the same?

Name: _____   Date: _____

Living Sunlight Choreography Planning Guide *(cont.)*

Unison

Use all nine movements from the steps of photosynthesis. Draw or describe the formation you will use.

Use this chart to record the order you will perform the movements.

Step of Photosynthesis	Movement Description
1	
2	
3	
4	
5	
6	
7	
8	
9	

Name: _____ Date:_____

Living Sunlight Choreography Planning Guide *(cont.)*

Fan

Draw or describe the formation you will use for the Fan. Use all nine movements from the steps of photosynthesis.

Use this chart to record the order in which each student will perform their movement.

Step of Photosynthesis	Student Name
1	
2	
3	
4	
5	
6	
7	
8	
9	

Name: _____ Date: _____

Living Sunlight Choreography Planning Guide *(cont.)*

Rondo

Use the movements from the steps of photosynthesis. Use this chart to record the order in which each student will perform movements.

Student A Sequence	Student B Sequence	Student C Sequence	Student D Sequence	Student E Sequence

Draw or describe the formation you will use to perform the movement sequence.

Name: _____ Date:_____

Living Sunlight Choreography Planning Guide *(cont.)*

Unison with Recurrence

Rewrite the movements from the steps of photosynthesis. Make sure to include a "twist" with at least two of the movements.

Draw a diagram that describes the sequence of the movements and how you will use Unison. What is the formation (circles, lines, or random)? Will the formation always be the same?

References Cited

Academy of American Poets. n.d. "Glossary of Poetic Terms." Accessed October 1, 2021. poets.org/glossary.

Alberts, Rebecca. 2008. "Discovering Science Through Art-Based Activities." *Beyond Penguins and Polar Bears.* The Ohio State University. beyondpenguins.ehe.osu.edu/issue/earths-changing-surface/discovering-science-through-art-based-activities.

Alexander, Kwame. 2019. *The Write Thing.* Huntington Beach, CA: Shell Education.

Alter, Charlotte, Syun Haynes, and Justin Worland. 2019. "Person of the Year 2019—Greta Thunberg." *Time*, December 2019. time.com/person-of-the-year-2019-greta-thunberg/.

Andersen, Christopher. 2004. "Learning in 'As-If' Worlds: Cognition in Drama in Education." *Theory into Practice* 43 (4): 281–286.

Anderson, Lorin W., David R. Krathwohl, Peter W. Airasian, Kathleen A. Cruikshank, Richard E. Mayer, Paul R. Pintrich, James Raths, and Merlin C. Wittrock. 2000. *A Taxonomy for Learning, Teaching, and Assessing: A Revision of Bloom's Taxonomy of Educational Objectives.* Boston: Allyn & Bacon.

Association of College and Research Libraries. 2011. "ACRL Visual Literacy Competency Standards for Higher Education." www.ala.org/acrl/standards/visualliteracy.

Baker, Beth. 2012. "Arts Education." *CQ Researcher* 22: 253–276.

Bamberger, Jeanne. 2000. "Music, Math, and Science: Towards an Integrated Curriculum." *Journal for Learning through Music Summer* 2000: 32–35.

Bang, Molly, and Penny Chisholm. 2009. *Living Sunlight: How Plants Bring the Earth to Life.* New York: Blue Sky Press.

Bellisario, Kerrie, and Lisa Donovan with Monica Prendergast. 2012. "Voices from the Field: Teachers' Views on the Relevance of Arts Integration." Unpublished manuscript. Cambridge, MA: Lesley University.

The Bindery. n.d. "What Is a Zine?" Accessed June 9, 2021. www.binderymke.com/what-is-a-zine.

Bodensteiner, Kirsten. 2019. "Do You Wanna Dance? Understanding the Five Elements of Dance." The Kennedy Center. www.kennedy-center.org/education/resources-for-educators/classroom-resources/media-and-interactives/media/dance/do-you-wanna-dance/.

Braund, Martin, and Michael J. Reiss. 2019. "The 'Great Divide': How the Arts Contribute to Science and Science Education." *Canadian Journal of Science, Mathematics and Technology* 19: 219–236. link.springer.com/article/10.1007/s42330-019-00057-7.

Brice-Heath, Shirley, with Adelma Roach. 1999. "Imaginative Actuality: Learning in the Arts During the Nonschool Hours." In *Champions of Change: The Impact of the Arts on Learning*, edited by Edward B. Fiske. Washington, DC: President's Committee on the Arts and the Humanities.

Bruce, Eloise, Maureen Heffernan, Sanaz Hojreh, Wendy Liscow, Shawna Longo, Michelle L. Marigliano, Erica Nagel, et al. 2020. *New Jersey's Arts Integration Think and Do Workbook: A Practical Guide to Think about and Implement Arts Integration.* Morristown, NJ: Geraldine R. Dodge Foundation. njpsa.org/documents/ArtsIntLdshpInst2020/artsintegrationWorkbook2020.pdf.

Cahill, Bryon. 2006. "Ready, Set, Write!" *Writing* 29 (1): 12.

Cappiello, Mary Ann, and Erika Thulin Dawes. 2013. *Teaching with Text Sets.* Huntington Beach, CA: Shell Education.

Carpenter, Siri. 2011. "Body of Thought: How Trivial Sensations Can Influence Reasoning, Social Judgment, and Perception." *Scientific American Mind*, January 2011, 38–45.

Cash, Justin. n.d. "The 12 Dramatic Elements." *The Drama Teacher* (blog). Accessed October 1, 2021. thedramateacher.com/wp-content/uploads/2008/02/The-12-Dramatic-Elements.pdf.

Center for Applied Special Technology. n.d. "About CAST." Accessed October 10, 2012. www.cast.org/about/index.html.

Ciecierski, Lisa, and William Bintz, 2012. "Using Chants and Cadences to Promote Literacy Across the Curriculum: Chants and Cadences Engage Students in Creative Writing and Critical Thinking." *Middle School Journal* 44 (2): 22–29. DOI:10.2307/41763116.

Collins, Polly. 2008. "Using Poetry throughout the Curriculum." *Kappa Delta Pi Record* 44 (2): 81–84.

Coulter, Cathy, Charles Michael, and Leslie Poynor. 2007. "Storytelling as Pedagogy: An Unexpected Outcome of Narrative Inquiry." *Curriculum Inquiry* 37 (2): 103–122.

Crowther, Gregory J., Tom McFadden, Jean S. Fleming, and Katie Davis. 2016. "Leveraging the Power of Music to Improve Science Education." *International Journal of Science Education* 38 (1): 73–95.

Dacey, Linda, and Jayne Bamford Lynch. 2007. *Math for All: Differentiating Instruction, 3–5.* Sausalito, CA: Math Solutions.

Dahlstrom, Michael F. 2014. "Using Narratives and Storytelling to Communicate Science with Nonexpert Audiences." *Proceedings of the National Academy of Sciences* 111 (Supplement 4): 13614–13620.

DBI Network. n.d. "Drama-Based Instruction: Guided Imagery." Accessed October 12, 2020. dbp.theatredance.utexas.edu/content/guided-imagery.

Diaz, Gene, Lisa Donovan, and Louise Pascale. 2006. "Integrated Teaching through the Arts." Presentation given at the UNESCO World Conference on Arts Education, Lisbon, Portugal, March 8, 2006.

Donovan, Lisa, and Louise Pascale. 2022. *Integrating the Arts Across the Curriculum, Second Edition.* Huntington Beach, CA: Shell Education.

Eisner, Elliot. 2002. "What the Arts Do for the Young." *School Arts* 102: 16–17.

Elliott-Johns, Susan E., David Booth, Jennifer Rowsell, Enrique Puig, and Jane Paterson. 2012. "Using Student Voices to Guide Instruction." *Voices from the Middle* 19 (3): 25–31.

References Cited *(cont.)*

Estrella, Espie. 2019. "An Introduction to the Elements of Music." *LiveAbout*. November 4, 2019. www.liveabout.com/the-elements-of-music-2455913.

Facing History and Ourselves. n.d. "Found Poems." Accessed August 9, 2021. www.facinghistory.org/resource-library/teaching-strategies/found-poems.

Faulkner, Sandra L., and Abigail Cloud, eds. 2019. *Poetic Inquiry as Social Justice and Political Response.* Wilmington, DE: Vernon Press.

Fox, David Charles. 2017. "What Is Installation Art? Description, History, and Prominent Artists." davidcharlesfox.com/what-is-installation-art-description-history-and-prominent-artists/.

Gardner, Howard. 2011. *Frames of Mind: The Theory of Multiple Intelligences*. 3rd ed. New York: Basic Books.

Glatstein, Jeremy. 2019. "Formal Visual Analysis: The Elements and Principles of Composition." The Kennedy Center. www.kennedy-center.org/education/resources-for-educators/classroom-resources/articles-and-how-tos/articles/educators/formal-visual-analysis-the-elements-and-principles-of-compositon/.

Governor Donna, Jori Hall, and David Jackson. 2013. "Teaching and Learning Science Through Song: Exploring the Experiences of Students and Teachers." *International Journal of Science Education*. 35 (18): 3117–3140. DOI: 10.1080/09500693.2012.690542.

Griss, Susan. 1994. "Creative Movement: A Language for Learning." *Educational Leadership* 51 (5): 78–80.

Growney, JoAnne. 2009. "What Poetry Is Found in Mathematics? What Possibilities Exist for Its Translation?" Mathematical Intelligencer 31 (4): 12–14.

Hamilton, Martha, and Mitch Weiss. 2005. *Children Tell Stories: Teaching and Using Storytelling in the Classroom*. Katonah, NY: Richard C. Owen Publishers.

Harmon, Wynita. 2018. "Teach Your Students to Observe Like Artists in Just 5 Steps." Osage, IA: The Art of Education University. theartofeducation.edu/2018/01/05/teaching-students-observe-like-artist-just-5-steps/.

Heard, Georgia. 1999. *Awakening the Heart: Exploring Poetry in Elementary and Middle School*. Portsmouth, NH: Heinemann.

Heathcote, Dorothy, and Gavin Bolton. 1995. *Drama for Learning: Dorothy Heathcote's Mantle of the Expert Approach to Education*. Portsmouth, NH: Heinemann.

Herman, Corie. 2003. "Teaching the Cinquain: The Quintet Recipe." *Teachers & Writers* 34 (5): 19–21.

Hershenhorn, Erin. 2020. "Wednesday Writing Workout: Word Bowl Poems." *Teaching Authors* (blog), April 15, 2020. www.teachingauthors.com/2020/04/wednesday-writing-workout-word-bowl.html?m=1.

Hetland, Lois. 2009. "Nilaja Sun's 'No Child' Revealing Teaching and Learning through Theater." *Teaching Artist Journal* 7 (1): 34–39.

Hetland, Lois, Ellen Winner, Shirley Veenema, and Kimberly Sheridan. 2007. *Studio Thinking: The Real Benefits of Visual Arts Education*. New York: Teachers College Press.

Hipp, Jamie, and Margaret-Mary Sulentic Dowell. 2021. "Arts Integrated Teacher Education Benefits Elementary Students and Teachers Alike." *EdNote* (blog), February 1, 2021. ednote.ecs.org/arts-integrated-teacher-education-benefits-elementary-students-and-teachers-alike/.

Hollander, John. 2014. "Speaking Pictures: Poetry Addressing Works of Art." National Gallery of Art. www.nga.gov/audio-video/audio/poetry-hollander.html.

Hourcade, Juan Pablo, Benjamin B. Bederson, and Allison Druin. 2004. "Building KidPad: An Application for Children's Collaborative Storytelling." *Software: Practice & Experience* 34 (9): 895–914.

International School of Athens. n.d. "Drama Handbook." Accessed May 4, 2021. isa.edu.gr/files/319/Drama_Handbook.pdf.

Jacobsen, Daniel Christopher. 1992. *A Listener's Introduction to Music.* Dubuque, Iowa: Wm. C. Brown Publishers.

Jenkins, Henry. 2009. *Confronting the Challenges of Participatory Culture: Media Education for the 21st Century.* Cambridge, MA: The MacArthur Foundation.

Jensen, Eric. 2001. *Arts with the Brain in Mind.* Alexandria, VA: Association for Supervision and Curriculum Development.

Jensen, Eric P. 2008. *Brain-Based Learning: The New Paradigm of Teaching.* 2nd ed. Thousand Oaks, CA: Corwin Press.

J. Paul Getty Museum. n.d.-a. "Elements of Art." Accessed October 1, 2021. www.getty.edu/education/teachers/building_lessons/formal_analysis.html/.

J. Paul Getty Museum. n.d.-b. "Principles of Design." Accessed October 1, 2021. www.getty.edu/education/teachers/building_lessons/formal_analysis2.html

Keillor, Garrison. 2006. "Samurai Song." *The Writer's Almanac,* October 20, 2006. writersalmanac.publicradio.org/index.php%3Fdate=2006%252F10%252F20.html

Kennedy, Randy. 2006. "Guggenheim Study Suggests Arts Education Benefits Literacy Skills." *New York Times,* July 27, 2006.

KET. 2014. "Principles of Design." PBS Learning Media. pbslearningmedia.org/resource/459077ac-6d7d-4eef-bd7e-e38d12e7ce97/principals-of-design/

Kozubek, Jim. 2018. "The Future of Science Storytelling." *Scientific American,* April 30, 2018. blogs.scientificamerican.com/observations/the-future-of-science-storytelling.

KQED Art School. 2015. "The Five Elements of Dance." PBS Learning Media. pbslearningmedia.org/resource/d7fcd19b-ee9b-4d90-a550-833fbe22865c/the-five-elements-of-dance/.

Kuta, Katherine. 2003. "And Who Are You?" *Writing* 25 (5): 30–31.

LaBonty, Jan. 1997. "Poetry in the Classroom: Part I." *The Dragon Lode* 75 (3): 24–26.

Lane, Barry 1992. *After THE END: Teaching and Learning Creative Revision.* Portsmouth, NH: Heinemann.

References Cited (cont.)

Lansky, Bruce. 2015. "Poetry Theater: How to Make Poetry Fun for Young Readers and More Entertaining for Their Audience." *NERA Journal* 51(1).

Lyon, George Ella. 2010. "Where I'm From." www.georgeellalyon.com/where.html.

Mantle of the Expert. n.d. "How Does MoE Work?" Accessed July 23, 2021. www.mantleoftheexpert.com/what-is-moe/how-does-moe-work/.

Marzano, Robert J. 2007. *The Art and Science of Teaching: A Comprehensive Framework for Effective Instruction.* Alexandria, VA: Association for Supervision and Curriculum Development.

Mason, Betsy. 2019. "Why Scientists Need to Be Better at Data Visualization." *Knowable Magazine*, November 12, 2019. knowablemagazine.org/article/mind/2019/science-data-visualization.

McCandless, David. 2010. "David McCandless: The Beauty of Data Visualization." TEDGlobal. www.ted.com/talks/david_mccandless_the_beauty_of_data_visualization.html.

McKim, Elizabeth, and Judith W. Steinbergh. 1992. *Beyond Words: Writing Poems with Children: A Guide for Parents and Teachers.* Brookline, MA: Talking Stone Press.

Merriam-Webster. n.d. "Collage." Accessed June 10, 2021. www.merriam-webster.com/dictionary/collage.

National Coalition for Core Arts Standards. 2014. "Glossary of Terms: Theatre." docplayer.net/29830664-Glossary-for-national-core-arts-theatre-standards.html.

National Research Council. 2012. *A Framework for K–12 Science Education: Practices, Crosscutting Concepts, and Core Ideas.* Washington, DC: The National Academies Press.

National Storytelling Network. n.d. "What Is Storytelling?" Accessed April 30, 2021. storynet.org/what-is-storytelling/.

Neelands, Jonothan, and Tony Goode. n.d. "Guided Imagery." *Drama-Based Instruction: Activating Learning through the Arts.* dbp.theatredance.utexas.edu/content/guided-imagery.

Norfolk, Sherry, Jane Stenson, and Diane Williams. 2006. *The Storytelling Classroom.* Westport, CT: Libraries Unlimited.

Oliver, Mary, 1994. *A Poetry Handbook: A Prose Guide to Understanding and Writing Poetry.* Orlando, FL: Mariner Books.

O'Neill, Cecily. 1995. *Drama Worlds: A Framework for Process Drama.* Portsmouth, NH: Heinemann.

Panckridge, Jo. 2020. "Storytelling: The Power of Oral Narratives." *Practical Literacy* 25(3).

Partnership for 21st Century Learning. 2019. "Framework for 21st Century Learning." static.battelleforkids.org/documents/p21/P21_Framework_Brief.pdf.

PBS NewsHour. 2019. "Climate Activist Greta Thunberg on the Power of a Movement." www.pbs.org/video/climate-warrior-1568414322/.

Perpich Center for Arts Education. 2009. "The Elements of Dance." www.nationalartsstandards.org/sites/default/files/Dance_resources/ElementsOfDance_organizer.pdf.

References Cited (cont.)

Perret, Peter, and Janet Fox. 2006. *A Well-Tempered Mind: Using Music to Help Children Listen and Learn.* New York: Dana Press.

Poetry Foundation. n.d. "Glossary of Poetic Terms." www.poetryfoundation.org/learn/glossary-terms.

Pope, Susan. n.d. "Science Drama Lessons." Accessed July 23, 2021. susanpope.com/lesson-plans/science-drama-lessons.html.

President's Committee on the Arts and the Humanities. 2011. "Reinvesting in Arts Education: Winning America's Future Through Creative Schools." www.pcah.gov/sites/default/files/PCAH_Reinvesting_4web_0.pdf.

Reed, Stephen K. 2010. *Cognition: Theories and Application.* 8th ed. Belmont, CA: Wadsworth Cengage Learning.

Reeves, Douglas. 2007. "Academics and the Arts." *Educational Leadership* 64 (5): 80–81.

Rhode Island School of Design. 2011. "Gathering STEAM in Rhode Island." www.risd.edu/About/News/Gathering_STEAM_in_RI/.

Riley, Susan. 2017. "The Elements of Art Anchor Charts." Institute for Arts Integration and STEAM. July 1, 2017. artsintegration.com/2017/07/01/elements-art-anchor-charts/.

Rinne, Luke, Emma Gregory, Julia Yarmolinskyay, and Mariale Hardiman. 2011. "Why Arts Integration Improves Long-Term Retention of Content." *Mind, Brain, and Education* 5 (2): 89–96.

Rose, Todd. 2012. "Learner Variability and Universal Design for Learning." *Universal Design for Learning Series.* udlseries.udlcenter.org/presentations/learner_variability.html.

Schafer, R. Murray. 1992. *A Sound Education.* Indian River, ON: Arcana Editions.

Scharner, Samara. 2019. "Storytelling for Oral Language Fluency." *Practical Literacy* 24 (2). link.gale.com/apps/doc/A589966989/AONE?u=mlin_w_masscol&sid=AONE&xid=66f37e35.

School Curriculum and Standards Authority. 2014. "Drama Elements." k10outline.scsa.wa.edu. au/home/teaching/curriculum-browser/the-arts/visual-arts2/arts-overview/glossary/elements-of-drama#.

Segaren, Sharuna. 2019. "Is Arts Integration in Schools All It's Cracked Up To Be?" *Study International*, January 14, 2019. www.studyinternational.com/news/is-arts-integration-in-schools-all-its-cracked-up-to-be/.

Skoning, Stacey. 2008. "Movement in Dance in the Inclusive Classroom." *TEACHING Exceptional Children Plus* 4 (6). files.eric.ed.gov/fulltext/EJ967723.pdf.

Strauch-Nelson, Wendy J. 2011. "Book Learning: The Cognitive Potential of Bookmaking." *Teaching Artist* 9 (1): 5–15.

Tate. n.d. "Art Term: Composition." Accessed June 9, 2021. www.tate.org.uk/art/art-terms/c/composition.

Varlas, Laura. 2012. "It's Complicated: Common Core State Standards Focus on Text Complexity." *Education Update* 54 (4).

References Cited *(cont.)*

Venkat, Srividhya. 2020. "Using Oral Storytelling Techniques in Reading Sessions." *Knowledge Quest* 48 (5).

Walker, Elaine, Carmine Tabone, and Gustave Weltsek. 2011. "When Achievement Data Meet Drama and Arts Integration." *Language Arts* 88 (5).

Ward, Sarah J., Rebecca M. Price, Katie Davis, and Gregory J. Crowther. 2018. "Songwriting to Learn: How High School Science Fair Participants Use Music to Communicate Personally Relevant Scientific Concepts." *International Journal of Science Education*, Part B. 8 (4): 307–324. DOI: 10.1080/21548455.2018.1492758.

Windmill Theatre Company. n.d. "Elements of Drama." Accessed October 1, 2021. windmill.org.au/wp-content/uploads/2018/09/Elements-of-Drama.pdf.

Yellin, David, Mary Blake Jones, and Beverly A. DeVries. 2007. *Integrating the Language Arts*. Scottsdale, AZ: Holcomb Hathaway Publishers.

Zhu, Lian, and Yogesh Goyal. 2019. "Art and Science: Intersections of Art and Science through Time and Paths Forward." *Science and Society* 20 (2). doi.org/10.15252/embr.201847061.

Zull, James E. 2002. *The Art of Changing the Brain: Enriching Teaching by Exploring the Biology of Learning*. Sterling, VA: Stylus.

Digital Resources

Accessing the Digital Resources

The digital resources can be downloaded by following these steps:

1. Go to **www.tcmpub.com/digital**

2. Use the ISBN to redeem the digital resources.

   > **ISBN 978-0-7439-7023-5**

3. Respond to the question using the book.

4. Follow the prompts on the Content Cloud website to sign in or create a new account.

5. Choose the digital resources you would like to download. You can download all the files at once, or a specific group of files.

Please note: Some files provided for download have large file sizes. Download times for these larger files vary based on your internet speed.